The Algorithm of Consciousness

KENNETH A MACFARLANE

ASHEVILLE NORTH CAROLINA USA

ISBN: 978-1-09833-613-4 (print)
ISBN: 978-0-57871-689-3 (eBook)
Publisher: BookBaby.com
Publisher Number For Title Management is: 1984257

Cover photography by: dawnfirephotography.com
Cover design by: lasmithproductions.com

Library of Congress Control Number: 2018675309
Printed in the United States of America

A brief definition

The use of the words **algorithm** and **consciousness** in the title is deliberately evocative. Why? An algorithm is typically defined as an abstract mathematical term constructed by humans. In contrast, the body is a living organic algorithm constructed by Divine Intelligence (The Mother/Father/Godforce).

Consciousness is a term open to multiple interpretations but has defied all attempts to pinpoint its origins. I propose that our body is the receptive temple through which consciousness facilitates the flow of self-awareness. The divine purpose? It is the subject of this book.

Preface

My purpose is to speak from a place of neutral balance

and share from that unconditional loving space.

I am learning to accept the gift of every day.

Sometimes, these gifts are wrapped in sorrow, grief, fear, and anger.

Others are wrapped in love, compassion, grace, and connection.

All gifts have one purpose:

opening my heart to allow

COMPASSION

For all

BEINGS

Acknowledgments

I have been fortunate to be surrounded by lovely talented folk who believed in my quest and encouraged me to reach deep for my authentic best. I want to express my sincere gratitude to Grace Wormwood; without her loving presence and persistence, I may not have been here to create this work.

Thank you, Janet Iris Sussman, for permitting me to cherry-pick quotes from *The Reality of Time*. The cosmology presented in her book was the framework on which I weaved my tapestry of imagination and intuition.

No writer can ever achieve success without the help of people willing to tell them the objective truth. I am grateful to Laura Weist for her loving persistence to detail and flow. Anita Giaimo is the best kind of fan; thank you.

An old Chinese proverb states, '*When sleeping women wake, mountains move.*' The following women are awake, and I am grateful for their creative support. Kelly Struder, Mairi Campbell, Allyson Zimmermann, Grace Wormwood, and Christel Veraart.

Four friends, in particular, have been a constant source of support. Jeremy Rabuck, Sonja Korner, Vic Kirby, and Marianne Kilkenny. You all listened with patience to my convoluted stories and personal challenges.

My thanks to all my old friends in Scotland for their support throughout my moments of doubt

Numerous others helped me identify small pieces of the jigsaw, without which the picture would not have been complete. You know who you are, thank you.

Finally, my heartfelt thanks to Linda Rose Macfarlane *for just being her magnificent self to the end. R.I.P*

Introduction

These essays offer my reflections on how to raise your awareness to a level where life's contradictions, confusions, and challenges can be viewed through a lens of understanding and empower you with a new sense of purpose.

Taking stock of my life, I recognize that the development of self-awareness has been a priority. In my early years, my reluctance to step forward and grasp life's opportunities frustrated both my teachers and me. I was hypersensitive, always aware of external signals, which made me contract into myself. I found this shrinking occurred because of a subconscious urge to be safe and accepted; with that awareness, I began the archeological dig to uncover the source of the emotional knots thwarting my authentic self's flowering.

Our past is unchangeable, yet memories can exert an undue influence on how we make decisions in the present moment. I was in my forties before realizing the undue influence the past exerted in my daily life. In one of these "aha" moments, I suddenly saw that any perceived sense of abandonment provoked my passive-aggressive behavior. To uncover the source of these emotions, I began to peel back the layers of unconscious patterns covertly interfering with my ability to stay in the present.

My wife bore the brunt of the emotional turmoil that followed as I tried to uncover my young life's hidden layers. To alleviate my existential angst and frustration at my volatility, she persuaded me to enroll in a Hindu philosophy course at the Edinburgh School of Philosophy, Psychology and Language Sciences.

The school's mantra about living in the present intrigued me. In an early lecture, this statement captured me: *We cannot be what we observe;*

therefore, what we see about ourselves cannot be us! That assertion struck a chord. If I was not who I thought I was, who was I? I remember feeling a tingle run through my body. I wanted to learn more. It was the first time I realized I was more than just a 'body' with a functional brain. It became apparent to me that there was a new aspect of awareness just below the conscious level—an element which I had occasionally glimpsed, called intuition.

The God-given gift of self-awareness is the birthright of humanity. This gift, due to competing pressures of change in our lives, has been poorly deployed. Today, crisis after crisis arise because of a lack of perspective and the discernment of self-awareness. We desperately need to turn our full attention to developing them. Greed and fear have a firm grip on the tiller, and humanity's existing course is, at best, uncertain and, at worst, disastrous for us and the planet. Whether we like it or not, change is an unstoppable, forward-looking dynamic.

If you commit to considering this book's contents with an open mind, I can assure you that you will emerge with a new inner feeling of self-worth. You will begin to embrace patience and a sense of peace—the peace arises from knowing that you/we are not alone. The Divine is inside you. You are a volunteer. You have a purpose in this glorious, messy dance of action and reaction—a dance orchestrated by the Divine to facilitate our graduation into a full, equal partnership with our hearts and minds.

You will be able to pause and balance your thoughts and come to a place of neutrality and peace in your daily life interactions. I can vouch for this technique because the words I have contributed to these essays arose from that quiet place inside.

Prologue

When I look back at some of the belief systems I confronted as a youth, I can see why I was always skeptical about glib answers from religious teachings about our nature. My Christian-based society's prevalent belief is that we exist as an isolated and independent physical vehicle and that divine intelligence plays some ineffable and unidentifiable role.

I have come to know that my body is a metaphoric organic algorithm: a Temple of Awareness.

Our central nervous system can receive subtle impulses from sources on a causal level outside this domain of consciousness. The body is a transmitter and receiver capable of ingesting and outputting knowledge from a broad spectrum of intelligent sources throughout the Universe.

The body is not intelligent in its own right. The body is nothing without the intervention of outside intelligence. The degree of awareness that we can achieve directly correlates to the information retrieved from the causal level. In understanding that to be true for me, I became determined to increase awareness and develop my intuition.

This exchange is open to all of us. Everyone has had some intuition experience, often only realized in retrospect: "I wish I had followed my gut!" It took a few painful experiences resulting from not paying attention to my intuition (usually because its voice did not match my ego's idea of what I wanted) before I gave in and listened to my intuitive, quiet voice. As a result, I have become more proactive and responsible for how I direct my life. I do not need to look for or worship some outside God. I look to my source of the Divine within.

From this perspective, I offer three assertions, which underpin the essays that follow.

As a species, we face significant changes to our environment, which will, if left unchecked, see human life on Earth face near extinction.

Earth is sentient and will evolve whether or not we as guests take responsibility for our salvation. We live in a 3rd-dimensional reality that works based on contrast called duality. The ultimate aim is to raise our self-awareness to the point where we come into balance and transcend the illusional pull of right/wrong. It is the only course on offer at 'The University of Earth.'

Contents

Disclaimer

My extrapolations and conclusions drawn from the quotes in Janet Iris Sussman's book *The Reality of Time* should not be interpreted as a reflection or collaboration about our mutual views or purpose of *The Reality of Time*.

KENNETH A MACFARLANE

Author of *The Algorithm of Consciousness*

June 2020

Patterns and Coincidences

We each come into this world with a pre-determined set of patterns; addendums are then integrated initially through parental input, a subject I shall cover in the essay "The Potential of Our Children." Some people seem to feel or know their purpose from an early age. I wanted to be a long-distance truck driver, the first hint perhaps of my impulse to travel and explore. "Connection" is my dominant pattern. Many of the threads of connection I made have turned into ropes throughout my life, still tugging decades later. You might be thinking, what is remarkable about that? Simply that, none of them are my family members. My only relative is a first cousin once removed. Almost eighty percent of my connections are women, for reasons which will become clear as you read this book.

Here are some significant examples of patterns: Aged fifteen, in a used bookstore for the first time, I was attracted to a paperback called *Timeliner* by Charles Eric Maine.* I remember the opening sentence: "Will stepped out of the Time Kettle." That was the introduction to my passion for science fiction. The inside cover was dedicated "To Ken." Decades later, a book called *Timeshift* by Janet Iris Sussman was gifted to me by a lady who could not get her head around the content. For me, the material was a game-changer, not science fiction but science prediction. Finally, ten years ago, *The Reality of Time* by Janet Iris Sussman became the catalyst for these essays. Are these coincidences or patterns?

My life is full of such "coincidences." They have a pattern that has weaved a protective and nurturing thread through the structure of my life.

Carl Jung was an eminent and highly radical 19th-century psychologist. His theories revolutionized humanity's view of how the human mind works. Jung observed such patterns in his investigations and called them "synchronistic events." From this and other sources, I have compiled two laws which complement the idea of synchronicity. The first of these laws states that, *we attract into our lives people and experiences from which we have something to learn.*

Therefore, by definition, the right people are always on hand at the appropriate moment, if we care to look! And, on the basis that everything that happens has a purpose, the conclusion drawn from this law must be that all experiences and interactions are good, insofar as they present us with excellent learning opportunities.

The problem is that our ego can deliberately blind us; it says, *If it hurts me, it cannot be good for me.* The ego also manifests that another inner tyrant, hindsight; hindsight is a curse because it provokes negative questions. *I could have done that better; why didn't I?* or, *I am useless, I could not do it.* "Why didn't I?" is the ultimate puzzle. Guilt and low self-worth are behind this question, which brings me to the second of my two laws.

At the moment of action in the game of life, we can only act on the knowledge available to us in that instant; we are doing the best we can! The hindsight judgments we bring to bear about our actions are not available. That knowledge only arises as a consequence of the game. This fact applies to everything we do, even if we know we are doing wrong! In such moments, we do not have the energy to step aside from the emotion driving us. To put it another way, we do not know how to apply the "stop" mechanism.

The inherent nature of hindsight is self-denigration, which triggers the never-ending prattle of self-doubt. The chatter of the mind is an insidious and compelling enforcer of illusion.

Depends on Your Point of View.

Achieving inner balance and peace seems almost impossible in a world where fear, and the conflicts it creates, dominates our behavior. However, I feel we have reached the cusp of this immature phase, and the opportunity to take our next evolutionary jump is open.

For me, there is no better illustration of the present divergence between hearts and minds than the two quotes below. The first is by Jiddu Krishnamurti, an Indian philosopher, speaker, and writer. The second is by Wilfred Edward Salter Owen, MC, an English poet, and soldier.

> *"Only when your hearts are empty of things of the mind is there love. Then you will know what it is to love without separation, without distance, without time, without fear."*

> *"What passing bells for those who die as cattle? Only the monstrous anger of guns."*

Is reconciliation possible between the love of the heart and the anger of despair? I assure you it is possible. It all depends on your point of view.

I am responsible for all I create in life. At the same time, I cannot control external events. I most definitely can control how I react to them. I invoke the cup half full or half empty analogy. On hearing a bad luck story, I often think about how lucky I have been. Some folks seem to suffer disproportionately from trauma and bad luck.

> [1]*Individuals who experience their reality as inherently favorable and positive will often create their personal matrix from respondency rather than obstinacy. One must become friends with the flow of consciousness rather than attempt to block it through the fear and hesitancy that often accumulates in the recesses of the mind.*

A friend of mine has always been a gambler with life. He is the epitome of an out-of-control ego playing with a hand that no card player, regardless of the game, would "consciously" choose to lay on the table of life. Suffice to say, the last card he played has left this person comatose and critical after a horrific car accident. My prayers go out to him.

When lousy luck befalls someone, we deem to be friendly, helpful, and loving, our reaction is anger: anger that a God, or that some angel, did not intervene and save them. On the other hand, if we feel a person deserves all they get, we justify this judgment by declaring "they are playing out their bad karma"! Perhaps you will see this dichotomy in a new light when you read the next quote, particularly your role as a playwright.

[2]*We have an exciting role to play in creating the mirroring of our reality, but we can never be fully masters of the time array that feed the essential character of it. It is as if we can be playwrights but have no control over how an individual actor might singularly interpret his or her role.*

I love the opening, highlighting the positivity of our creative capability. My ego's proclaimed entitlement to speak as me has been a hard thing to recalibrate. I can tell you, freedom and peace are the rewards for dealing with this aspect of our humanity. I am happy to be the "playwright" and write my lines in cooperation with the flow of acceptance.

For most of us, change is not something we cherish, especially when change appears to be unpleasant, traumatic, or plain unfair. There are four prime imperatives which exert their protocols on how each of us experiences our existence in the human body: safety, survival, identity, and pain. The law of opposites (duality) states that every action creates an opposite position, e.g., right/wrong, good/bad, positive/negative; our reactions triggered at a subconscious level dramatically influence our behavior.

Bodies are vulnerable, and bodies need to be protected. Minds are fragile. Minds need anchors of stability to remain functional and have a sense of identity. Hence the four protocols mentioned above are embedded in the subconscious. Time, therefore, is experienced as being linear. Past, present, and future are the stimulants for our imagination. Fear, joy, love, and loving physical contact, like a magnet, attract the new, the spicy, the mundane, and the extraordinary. Look what humanity has achieved in service to others and, in turn, to self; these are positive and negative polarities. Is it any wonder we have existential angst?

> [3]Due to the feeling of terror evoked by randomization, human beings try to control their perceptual universe by creating conflict. This conflict mirrors the second governing law of time, which is the law of opposites.

Life is like trying to put a complex jigsaw puzzle together with no accurate picture of the final image. A jigsaw puzzle is a two-dimensional representation of three-dimensional objects. We incarnated into three-dimensional pieces of a multi-dimensional jigsaw. The Godforce constructs our three-dimensional body as an organic algorithm to realize our original purpose and potential for our incarnation. Unhooking ourselves from the tyranny of "linear time" has, up until now, been inappropriate because the untrained mind could not withstand the destabilization as can be amply demonstrated by the fear-fueled tragedies which dominate our journey throughout history. The Divine, wishing to gain experience in the 3D world of duality, created individuals who, using all their discernment, interpret, represent, delineate, and define the field of matter in which they exist. Let us say "the Divine" developed an optical feedback system registered in our visionary structure, which would allow us to "see" time daily. Furthermore, through a collaborative process, a process between our eyesight and our other alert senses, we come to know ourselves and our environment.

The fact that you are reading this essay, even if the content seems somewhat bizarre, is, in my opinion, a sign that you are ready to consider other realities, to find a better, more loving way of expressing the Divine in human form.

Earth: An Independent Sentient Being.

Uncomfortable scenarios for humankind to consider.

[1]The concept of a "spaceship Earth" wherein the Earth itself will travel, break free from this dimensional outpost, and understand its place in the full plan is something that is little understood now.

[2]We view Earth as an outpost for sentient life rather than conscious life itself.

[3]The planetary Intelligence is so strong, so mighty, and really inviolate in its operating mechanics that, although it may appear damaged, it is rarely injured by civilizations that act as matchbooks upon it. When the planet itself gets ready to ignite, it will take everything with it that is seemly and just leave behind that which it does not want.

Running through these essays are well-crafted words laying out what is at stake for our civilization if we do not change our ways and cast aside the illusionary cloak of self-grandiosity. Such a culture that acts without consideration for all sentient life *does not have a long "life" expectancy.*

The wheels of change are steamrolling over the jagged denials of climate change. Our disregard for other beings is there for all to see.

The stories about the dreadful fate of millions of creatures we call livestock who perished in the North Carolina floods of 2018 turned my stomach. I have long since given up meat, pork, and veal. I still eat turkey and fish. My point? I appreciate and understand how difficult it is to remove the cloak of habit from our shoulders.

When viewed from the perspective of the planet, our actions are equivalent to "matchbook fires." *The Earth will take the seemly on the next stage of evolution and leave all else behind!* Who or what will qualify as "seemly"? I choose to listen to my heart and intuition for answers.

With some trepidation, I concur with the scenario described below.

[4]*This is the function of the Mother or Host Intelligence. We must understand that the Mother is the principal compositor of the time/space relationship between matter and absolute causation. Therefore, the Mother does not need of retaining anything which is fairly toothless and unfree. She will rip apart all of Her creation for the purpose of restitution.*

The Mother is capable of tough love! A topic I will discuss later. Suffice to say, at this moment, we as a civilization have a lot to learn.

Our Status as a Civilization

The manifestation of humankind is a divine algorithm: a collective force of energy designed by "the Divine" to reach out and get to know itself better. Or to put it another way, God needs Man as much as Man needs God. In that respect, we are equal aspects of THE ONE.

Those who believe that human creation happened 5,000 years ago refute the timescale of evolution uncovered by scientific research. But I am sure we can agree that the building of the human body and infusing it with conscious awareness require Intelligence beyond anything we can understand.

Sitting in the opposite camp, we have such luminaries as Stephen Hawking[*] and Max Planck[†] They both made cogent scientific arguments that there is no God. While diversity has no limits to its expression, I find it difficult to subscribe to any belief system that does not acknowledge that Intelligence is orchestrating creation.

Although our philosophies play out differently in this melting pot of duality, we are each designed to follow a path lit by the light of our beliefs. It all boils down to recognizing we are all in this journey together and will not arrive until we fully embrace the thrust toward a vibrational shift into the fifth dimension.

In my last essay (Earth: An Independent Sentient Being), there is a quote about the ultimate creator/destroyer, the Mother/Host Intelligence. She takes no prisoners if civilizations interrupt the event sequences laid out

---

[*]   Stephen Hawking. 1942–2018. English theoretical physicist, author, and cosmologist

[†]   Max Planck. 1858–1947. German theoretical physicist and Nobel prize winner

in the cosmic planning room. The following quote clarifies my truth. You, of course, are free to make your assessment.

> [1]*This is how the time lords feel about civilizations at the level of ours. They rise and fall and take all their variables with them, and there is no reason to change or break them up unless they interfere with things as they are.*

For many of you, the concepts presented above will be familiar. Humanity has free will to play within the bubble of our reality.

Our species' metamorphosis is a long game planned and overseen by the light beings charged with caring for this section of the universe. I do think the MOTHER is assessing our readiness for another step forward as a species.

In 2005 Adidas created an advertisement with the words "Impossible is a big word used by small men." I try to match my decisions with that criterion in mind.

Golem and Pygmalion Effects

Humans are hardwired to mirror each other; how hard is it not to sneeze after a person close to you sneezes? The desire to imitate my group's behavior makes mirroring hard to resist. The Golem effect[‡] is the name given to negative mirroring. Positive mirroring, the Pygmalion effect,[§] is when we mimic uplifting behavior or action. As one of the first steps in achieving balance and compassion, the Pygmalion effect desperately needs to be re-enforced in humankind's daily life.

One could imagine that the universe is God's playground. After all, a playground is a place where all possibilities and games are considered appropriate. The rules of a new event or belief system are initially settled by consensus of the participants. These rules then become established and formalized and merge into the cultural mores of the tribe, group, or nation, and a fixed hierarchy emerges.

In the eighties, windsurfing in Scotland emerged as the "new game in town," and there was no established hierarchy. Our group was in the forefront, forming an association, clubs, and a competitive racing calendar. In effect, we were the original hierarchy, and I was appointed secretary of the largest club in Scotland. The established sailing fraternity tried to swat us like mosquitoes, stealing their lifeblood or, in this case, their assumed position as the dictators of etiquette on the sea. This new breed of sailors was young

---

‡ *The Golem effect is a psychological phenomenon in which lower expectations placed upon individuals either by supervisors or the individual themselves lead to poorer performance by the individual. This **effect** is mostly seen and studied in educational and organizational environments. Wikipedia

§ The **Pygmalion effect,** or Rosenthal effect, is the phenomenon whereby others' high expectations of a target person positively affects the target person's performance. The effect is named after the Greek myth of Pygmalion, a sculptor who fell in love with a statue he had carved, or alternately, after the psychologist Robert Rosenthal. Wikipedia

and enthusiastic. Nothing is more guaranteed to sound warning bells in the minds of the established power bases than youthful enthusiasm. Other elected members and I fell into the pattern of enacting rules to maintain the status quo.

Change is a complete anathema to power groups as they struggle to control the rules of their game. To achieve this goal, they tap into all humans' fundamental need to be "right." Creating divisiveness in the collective leads to the inevitable right/wrong and good/evil clashes that have devastated our history.

In my daily interactions, I hear myself voicing my collective group's views, making statements that emphasize difference and hatred. Afterward, I realize my behavior, which stemmed from my need to be accepted, had overwritten my profound disagreement with their divisive rhetoric. The strange thing is that individually, they wish, deep in their hearts, that a more inclusive loving way could come to pass. The pressure to be loved and accepted is not easy to overcome because our most significant social challenge is being out of step with our group's views. For example, if this book's unorthodox contents strongly resonate, you will probably find yourself at odds with even your nearest and dearest. You will have become a victim of "the Golem effect."

Perhaps including the need to be right in human beings is a deliberate act by the Godforce and can be characterized as the expression of the collective's desire to know God!

[1]*The desire of the individual to know God allows him or her to be captivated by the flow of Time. The individual learns that his or her subjective reality is made up of God's wishes and is not simply an outgrowth of his or her span of awareness. Out of service to God, the individual shirks the opportunity to go his or her own way and becomes responsible for leaning toward the flow of Time that he or she perceives is valuable to the infinite itself.*

Synchronicity a Tool of the Divine

One tangible manifestation qualifies as objective proof that a higher-order exists: synchronicity—the simultaneous occurrence of events that appear significantly related but have no discernible causal connection. When I look deeper and take a longer perspective about synchronistic events in my life, the outcomes, regardless of whether the actual event was pleasant, lead to new doors opening into potential rooms. I am being nudged or shoved onto a predetermined path to help me stay "on purpose." These nudges, in their extreme form, are what we call miracles. The creator of these phenomena is a higher Intelligence.

In the final analysis, scientific proof is of no importance in a journey that is highly personal. It is a journey of discovery, the search for the ability to be our true Self. It is a journey that requires more than intellect as a guide. The map of our route can only come through the inner knowledge available when we tune in to our intuition.

Intuition is not an elusive skill. It may be hard to distinguish its quiet voice, often drowned out by ego's loud demands. Because intuition's inaudible messages usually run contrary to the ego's strident desires, we ignore them. Disconcertingly, it is only in retrospect that the meaning of these messages generally becomes evident and easy to understand, much like a riddle whose purpose is "as clear as a bell" after resolution dawns.

Intuition is not complicated. The attribute we label "common sense" is the outer expression of intuition's urges. Our sense of ethical behavior has its origins in our intuition. I state this categorically in the knowledge that intuition directly links with The Oneness of the Whole.

I do not use the word God; for me, it is a word that implies that the Divine is a separate being. We are part of the Godhead or the Oneness of the Whole.

The biblical God is the creator of everything; how can anything be created by him/her be anything less than perfect? The answer is, we cannot. We are all interdependent parts of the Oneness of Whole, and Our higher Self is the expression of that part of us which remains perfect. Therefore, the only way to contact our higher Self is to go inwards to do so.

Plato stated that "knowledge brings freedom." I yearn for freedom. The irony is that I will only achieve freedom by accepting the jurisdiction that civil and spiritual law has in my life. Plato's writing awakened my appreciation of a new perspective on law and order. I have always resented the blunt instrument that is the law. My experiences with those charged with upholding the law have left me with the impression that such a duty necessitates the application of a cold, harsh, and often unfair ethos.

However, this view changed when I read Plato's story about Socrates. Having been found guilty of a capital offense, he insisted that he suffer the full consequences of the law. Socrates was a very influential person who could have negotiated a reduced sentence. Instead, he declared that as he fully expected the law to protect him in his daily life, he should not shrink from the responsibility to fulfill his side of the bargain. In standing by that statement, Socrates' displayed exceptional personal integrity. I honestly believe he had transcended and overcome the accident of his internal illumination.

[1]*An intelligence is born that is capable of perfect self-reflection without a subjective self to censor or capture time. A dancing floating sensation unpinned by the flow of the mind predominates. The body has to overcome the accident of internal illumination.*

¶   It may be presumptuous of me to guess at Socrates's state of mind, but he undoubtedly had transcended beyond the consciousness of ordinary human beings

Ripening the Fruit of Devotion and Surrender

Leaving behind all our precious stories, which have defined our identities, is not easy.

Each of us has had at least one existential "aha" moment. I want to share two events that reshaped and transformed a long-held spiritual attitude in me. I came to understand the gift of devotion comes only through attunement of the heart.

During a spiritual naming ceremony, the first event cherry-picked from a much larger story that will unfold in the next essay. Sarina, an American lady, told me I had to intuit my "angelic name" in preparation for a spiritual workshop in Edinburgh led by a mystic called Solara. Somewhat skeptical, I agreed to accompany her to her spiritual altar on Arthur's Seat, an extinct volcano that dominates Edinburgh's skyline.

With a voice as impressive as her physical presence, Sarina began to chant and dance in a circle. After about five minutes, during which time I sat praying, a crowd had formed, curious about this strange performance. Sarina stopped and said, "The time is right, clear your mind, and ask your Higher Self to reveal your angelic name." Despite my growing discomfort, a name immediately jumped into my consciousness. I tried to ignore it. It sounded pretentious and silly. At her request, I repeated *Solaris Amon Ra* three times at the same time, thinking about how presumptuous and predictable that I should choose a name so similar to Solara's.

Sarina declared Solaris Amon RA was highly appropriate. *"What does my name mean?"* I asked her. *"Well, you are related to the Sun and the house of the ancient god Amon RA. It's the intuitive remembrance of your spiritual heritage and star lineage."*

Sarina intuited that we should look for a sign in the sky to seal this naming ceremony. Still feeling a bit embarrassed about this now public performance and still skeptical, I did not follow her expansive gesture as she raised her arms skyward. Within a few seconds, she began to shout, *"My God. My God!"* I followed the line of her frantically pointing finger. *"Bloody hell, there is something strange up there!"* Others nearby transfixed were looking upward.

High up in a clear blue sky, a figure-like shape was undulating, unlike any cloud formation. It was translucent, but, despite myself, I could see it looked like a vast winged being, an angel! My legs started to give; my heart was pounding; was this indeed Divine intervention? Was this to be the fulfillment of my most ardent wish to have a live experience of a Divine intervention/message? My legs were trembling, and I fell to my knees in a state of complete awe and surrender. Sarina was chanting; others, strangers, were standing open-mouthed. It was apparent they too thought they were in the presence of something not of this Earth.

Astounded, we watched in silence as this vision moved slowly away but retained the essence of its shape. A voice suddenly cried out in an authoritative tone, *"Balloons, extremely high are making the shape.* This news, delivered by a man gazing through binoculars, shattered the awed atmosphere. I was both disappointed and relieved. Even though the nature of our purpose seemed to suggest the possibility of such a miraculous conclusion, it scared me. Sarina exclaimed, *"Hell, balloons they may have been, but it was still a sign."* In one respect, she was right: The explanation for the physical manifestation was in itself unimportant. The sighting had been a significant moment for all of us. I did not know I was capable of such intense anticipation and such fervent hope. The intensity of wonder will always remain with me.

When the heart is the engine of awareness, our energy field softens. Here is my example. While meditating in a quiet spot in the local bird sanctuary, I became aware of a presence. I opened my eyes to find a wren sitting on the bench about six inches away from me. We looked at each other, then surprisingly, it hopped onto my knee and perched for several minutes. He fluttered off, then came back ten minutes later and hovered about six inches away from my face before settling on the bench's arm. I shed tears of gratitude.

> [1]*However, in the more aware or conscious individual, the gates of memory have been stripped so that more of what is known to be essentially true or accurate in the context of the individual's soul stream can come online.*

Doorways to Cognition

What is cognition? It is the process of knowing, gaining knowledge through reasoning, experience, and introspection: all skills I wanted to master. I found that meditation was the best method to challenge the tyranny of the ego. The main obstacle to inner quietness was the invasive chattering inside my head. Aided by fear or worry, the mind's prattle is an insidious and compelling enforcer of illusion.

In 1987 I enrolled in a twelve-week course "Exploring the Nature of Man" offered by the Edinburgh School of Philosophy. The course material asserted that *our ego is responsible for fostering the false opinions and beliefs that drive most of our actions. To find our real purpose for being alive, we have to shatter the illusion about our lives that these falsehoods promote.* This statement is relevant in the 21st century.* The twelve-week course turned into five transforming years of deeply committed inner work.

In 1991, I could no longer ignore my strong intuitive urge to say goodbye to gurus and teachers' peddling passive devotion. I needed to spread my wings.

A paperback with a white glossy and a golden starburst embossed on the front cover caught my eye as a beam of sunlight lit it up. The title similarly embossed in gold read, "Star-Borne 11:11." The author Solara is an American spiritual teacher, author, channel, and quantum healer. Something about the book's energy struck a chord in me; it exuded an air of mystical charisma. I decided to invite Solara to give a workshop in Edinburgh. (This was before my name initiation ceremony I talked about in the last essay.)

"First Connection" was an event planning group run by some lovely volunteers and me. My mission was to provide a selection of alternative spiritual speakers to Edinburgh. Solara was the perfect person to invite. Venue cancellations and surprise reinstatements appeared at first to be insurmountable, but I could sense a pattern: there was a higher purpose unfolding, so I stepped into its flow! A flow that would introduce me to all the people that were to become significant players in my life during the following eighteen months.

Solara called me to the Egyptian pyramids to assist her in a ceremony to be held on 11th January 1992, heralding in the energetic opening of the first of eleven spiritual ascension doors: part of an unfolding progression culminating on 11th January 2012. Over 500 folks answered the call of the 11:11 to elevate humanity into what Solara called a "New Octave of Oneness."

Creating group awareness required an immense amount of discipline and self-love. What started as the five hundred individuals transformed into a community with one goal of bringing love equally to all beings. It is as the following quotes from Dr. Sue Morter, a spiritual warrior and advocate for evolution, illustrate.

"Humanity is evolving, and each of us plays an important part in the direction in which it progresses. With every thought, action, and intention, we have the power to affect the world around us. One of the most powerful actions we can make is committing to our unique acts of outrageous love that come from our true heart's desire."

"Outrageous acts of love also demand courageous acts of commitment to break free of the shackles imposed by our human conditioning."

I became aware that I had treated my past meditation practice as a competitive event. Egotistic kudos had been based on who had meditated longer, had the most amazing experiences, or had achieved individual recognition from the spiritual leader. Whereas creating outrageous acts of love demands a state of BEING: A minute by minute devotion to seeing ALL as equals, and in need of loving acceptance. This journey is not comfortable.

Every day, the friction and contrast awash in this world cause judgments and assumptions to vault into the forefront of my mind waving the sword or banner of anger, fear, and self-righteousness. Patience is required to allow the process of breaking down societal conditioning and being open to the heart and intuition.

The litmus test of a heart-based decision is that you never need to justify your actions. Messages from intuition are authentic personal truths transmitted from a multi-dimensional source.

[3]*The individual essentially dies to the infantile identity*** *and becomes capable of developing a temporal landscape at once original, uniform, and synchronous with the underlying capabilities of the body.*

**   *To paraphrase: We are held at bay by the infantile mechanics that originally took place in our childhood.

No "Me": The Gift of Surrender?

One of the basic tenets of enlightenment is choosing to surrender one's ego-personality and the false sense of freedom it engenders. How much easier would the choice be if we would accept that our freedom lies in realizing we are not alone? Humanity is a fledgling partner of a multi-dimensional community under the God force's auspices, the universal intelligence, the infinite being, or whatever alias you wish to address the "divine, ineffable presence."

I spent most of my formative years, unaware of how much ego's desires dominated my behavior, which often led to sorrow and conflict. My emotional outlook was childish, not childlike. My ego was in charge, and it needed to get what it wanted!

The quote below from Ken Wilbur* was the catalyst that opened my heart to the gift of surrender.

The great You, the great Thou, the radiant, living, all giving God before whom I must surrender in love and devotion and sacrifice and release. In the face of Spirit in the 2nd person, in the face of the God who is ALL LOVE."

The words *God before whom I must surrender* sent me into a fit of righteous anger, and I blurted out, *"No way will you get me to become a devotee and surrender to some God."* My whole body shook in shock and rejection. I was sure the answers lay outside myself. In my ignorance, I had jumped to the conclusion that *the all-giving God* Wilbur was referring to a separate external entity. It is the God force inside each of us to whom we need to surrender.

The meaning of the "great Thou" is now exact and alive for me. The key to unlocking the "great Thou" in ourselves lies dormant within our central nervous system. All of us have *a great Thou* but recognizing that identity requires a colossal surrender and heart-opening. The heart is the place where reason is softened and made pliable.

My ego's basic sketch that hangs in the gallery of my consciousness achieves importance because of its illusional, glittering gold-plated border. However, like the story of how the clear eye of a child exposed the "Emperor's new suit*††" as being invisible, the clear self-reflection of humankind will reveal the real purpose of the ego as a servant rather than a leader.

> [1]*Once the individual leaves behind the need to catalyze his or her own existence and identity as being something special or different, then he or she can truly come into the realm of the infinite being.*

The patterns of nature are shining examples of surrender. The forces of death and renewal do not work in isolation; they weave together to achieve balance and growth. And, one can see that in the long-term, there is a balance at play. Nature is pragmatic. She deals with the need of the moment without hesitation, as the following quote alludes too.

> [2]*One sees how Nature creates life as well as how it destroys it. One no longer wishes to interfere with this process, but by understanding how it has come about one finds a sense of renewed peace.*

Despite as a teenager working on my father's farm, my relationship with Nature was controversial and delicate. I did not want to take over the business. I felt to do so would restrict my desires. I was a big city boy. In retrospect, I look back with gratitude. I loved working with the animals, and that love opened my eyes to the beauty of Nature that nurtures all beings. I have reached a balanced heartfelt perspective on the situation presented in the quote; I have a sense of renewed peace.

---

†† *The Emperor's New Clothes* by Hans Christian Anderson. Printed: 1837

Breath: The Elixir of Awakening

¹*The recognition of the breath as the key mechanism for the awakening of consciousness forms the backdrop for physical and emotional health. The health of the mind depends on the intake of subtle breath.*

A woman sitting across from me in the YMCA sauna attracted my attention; she was performing a series of coordinated movements using her hands, breath, and body. When I exited the sauna some fifteen minutes later, she was still going through the same ritual. I waited; I was curious. Eventually, she emerged, and I grasped the opportunity to speak to her. I asked if she was performing a style of yogi breathing technique. Smiling, she said, "*No, I don't follow any yogi. I just listened to my intuition and developed this sequence of breathing and bodywork. I find it has changed my life for the better.*"

I was surprised and delighted; here was a living example of the subject of this essay. I said, "*Well done. I am glad you follow your heart and intuition.*" She agreed, smiled, and the conversation was over. It was a synchronous moment. A reaffirmation that there are no coincidences in this life!

One thing is sure, this journey to "full potential" involves extracting myself from my ingrained habits, following a path which many label otherworldly, takes courage to go against the urge to be part of the tribe. Ironically, learning to breathe correctly is accepted and encouraged in all holistic practices.

²*Whole empires or star civilizations are based on this conceptual knowledge. Those civilizations that have mastered the breath of*

22

primary unification, therefore, can live independently of even a planetary system or civilization.

There is hope for humanity. Every breath is spiritual, and every event is a guide and a gift. My body, as well as my mind, must be cared for and nurtured. The quote below addresses this point.

[3]*When a being is born to this dimension; the soul is infused with a calendar in which is written the approximate time that this soul will be incarnated on the Earth plane.*

These words reinforce the argument for optimizing the quality of our life and letting go of what we cannot control. We can evolve from our "caterpillar" phase into "free-flying" multi-dimensional beings.

Memory: The Storehouse of Our Reality

An excellent article by Joshua Rothman appeared in the *New Yorker* magazine on November 12, 2018. The content pointed to a complex challenge facing humanity as the sophistication of image manipulation poses the question of what is real? As Rothman's article suggested, the problem is the word eyewitness is now an oxymoron.

Recently a video posted on Facebook received over a million views. It portrayed a small boy being snatched into the air by an eagle. It was fake, but that image is registered and regurgitated according to the viewer's memory and biases. If only 20 percent of viewers think the video is factual, around 200,000 people have a false opinion about eagles' nature and abilities.

The case above is a small example of the mounting challenges to our ability to discriminate between authentic and doctored images and videos. Evidence points to the assertion that we are evolutionarily predisposed to jump to conclusions: conclusions that confirm our views. These challenges could be a significant reason for the level of friction generated in the endeavor to facilitate the shift in consciousness required to move humanity into unity consciousness. I think the answer, in a different but relevant context, can be teased from the quote below about the trickle of event streams.

> [1]*Event streams trickle down from one plane of awareness to another, much like a waterfall leaves traces of itself on the rocks. These silent streams become powerful forces of reckoning when blended with the tributaries of consciousness that have already been established.*

Several years ago, I enjoyed a drink with a few friends, sitting comfortably around a table on which several glasses resided. Conversation and humor flowed only to be abruptly brought to an awed silence when a pint glass half full of beer shattered, showering beer over us. We sat open-mouthed for a few minutes, struggling to offer explanations. The conversation quickly sputtered out, and the subject dropped.

A few days later, only two of the seven who had been present still agreed that the glass had spontaneously shattered. The consensus was that one of us had hit the glass with our arm or hand. Looking back, I can take comfort from the following quote about memory having no experience categorizing the event.

> [2]*You do not have anything in your awareness that your memory cannot identify. If there is a new object, situation, or person, your ability to identify its existence is based solely on your past experience.*
>
> *If you cannot identify the nature of an object, then your brain simply switches off and returns the unidentifiable object to source… They have slipped into an area that your brain and central nervous system do not know how to catalogue.*

Outcomes like the one above all make sense to me as we (humanity) struggle to raise our vibration and awareness without being bogged down in the need to reason, understand, label, and judge. As the Russian philosopher Lev Shestov (1866–1938) wrote

> *Reason had to be overcome in order for us to know God.*
>
> *Revelation carries us beyond the limits of all human comprehension and of the possibilities that comprehension admits.*

Even with the expansion of my perspective, I find it challenging to stay balanced and compassionate as the bizarre, incomprehensible scenarios of human cruelty play out daily around the planet.

> [3]*Remember that everything we see on this plane is a registration of the brain and the central nervous system and is no more real than the dream images we see in our awareness in sleep. The difference is that they are more concrete; they are touchable. Why*

is this so? This is because we are congruent with them timewise and spatially. It is congruence renders them solid and opaque. They have no solidity in and of themselves.

I believe we are all doing our best with the information that our life experiences have imprinted in our memories.

Diminishing the Illusion

Codependency is not confined to enabling another person's addiction. Its most insidious manifestation is our codependency to our ego's story about who we are: an addiction that has trapped us in the illusion of separation for eons.

Breaking the energetic cords of attachment to an inner manager who presents a black and white agenda as being imperative for the survival of egoistic individuality does not happen because you think you understand why the ambiguity exists.

Mental analysis alone does not resolve behavioral fluctuations. Impulses of this nature are symptomatic of stronger hidden traumas orchestrating our behaviors. The solution is buried deep in our subconscious and carries a warning label; Opening this issue will cause pain: Requiring empathic professional support.

In my case, tearful episodes, spasms of fear, dread, or hopelessness compressing my gut stopped when I surrendered and allowed the toxicity to exit through emotional catharsis. I was then able to listen compassionately as the causes came to the surface. They were messages from my body alerting me that the pressure of keeping the murk trapped in quarantine was taking its toll.

At the age of three weeks, I was adopted and separated from my Mother. Unknown to me, the consequences of that trauma had flooded my emotional stability on many an occasion. Through the Jungian Shadow work process, I recovered the non-verbal distress simmering in my gut.

When the fear of abandonment, usually in relationships, overwhelmed my system, I turned into a passive-aggressive compliant needy person. I made many decisions through that prism of fear. I had no idea at the time a frightened inner child was running my adult life.

My passive-aggressive inner voice would issue dictates like, *"Why am I always the one who has to phone or connect with this person? No more, I am not doing that again. To hell with them!"* Alternatively, Mister ever helpful would emerge to serve their needs. Ironically that aspect of my behavior had many pluses in career and relationship.

My story that the urge to be 'helpful,' stemmed from a higher perspective, was false. My subconscious narrative was abandonment: *'if I don't reach out, nobody will come to me'*. At that moment, twenty-five years ago, I felt I had no sense of who I was or what I, as a unique, authentic being, wanted from life.

I do now.

All spiritual wisdom sources maintain that enlightenment comes through the surrender of our ego desires and quietening the turbulence of the mind. When we open to a Unity perspective, we can look back at our turbulence with compassion.

I was struck by how much the last two verses of a poem called 'Repetition' by Robert Pinsky, poet laureate of the United States 1997-2000, painted a perfect metaphor for my opening statement about codependence.

> *"The prophecy says you turn your back*
>
> *on the ocean* (the mind)
>
> *And lug your battered oar* (ego) *far inland,*
>
> *until*
>
> *You find a people who don't know what the quaint*
>
> *Artifact might be, although they may*
>
> *admire it*
>
> *As a relic of that ancient murmur, the ocean-*
>
> *Turbulent chorus of my dead, and all I want."*

Preparation

"Trauma imbeds pieces of emotional shrapnel in our cellular structure only to surface much later in life and are difficult to remove without help." (anon)

I have struggled to align with the contradictions of my humanity. I have always been mission-oriented at the expense of heart-based considerations. The living heart is an experience, not a concept.

For over five decades, my mission-based stubbornness has, on many occasions, overruled heart-based intuition.

In hindsight, the many clues, bumps, and emotional storms orchestrated by my guides were not enough to disrupt my fixed view of the roadmap.

Recently, driven, I guess by urgency, the guides changed tack and delivered their latest message in the shape of a teardrop rather than the usual emotional storm.

I woke one morning, open and vulnerable in a swirl of emotional turmoil. Through my tears (I cry easily), I became aware of a quiet but clear internal voice with a startling message, *"You are ready to start your spiritual journey. The life experiences you have has filled your internal library with a diverse selection of information about the many spiritual paths spread out across this planet's landscape. It is impossible to embark on a spiritual path until you have embraced and unconditionally love all aspects of yourself. This process is euphemistically known as 'The long dark night of the soul."*

The voice continued, *"Your heart has been closed, so it has not been possible to cleanse the many traumas stored in your cellular structure."*

The human body is an organic algorithm constructed to be the cradle in which consciousness births awareness of the material world. This instrument has the capability of transmitting and receiving wisdom and information across a broad spectrum of dimensions.

Since early childhood, I have known I had a purpose. I had seen Orbs and spheres of blinding white light, experiences often distressing, but they anchored my strong sense of curiosity and a feeling of being looked after.

Many decades ago, as an adult in the infancy of my existential angst, two provocative assertions resonated:-

> *'Everyone is doing the best they can at every moment, based on the information they have at that moment.'*
>
> *'You cannot see yourself; you can only BE yourself. It is impossible to be what you see, or what you think, in the same way as you cannot be anything you observe.'*

Today, I respect the autonomy of every living being.

I see these two assertions above as being mutually inclusive. If I do not like myself or see myself in a negative light, then these limiting beliefs will diminish the information available to me to make informed, intuitive decisions.

Each of us, whether we acknowledge it or not, are the masters of our destiny. We do have control over how we choose to react to external events.

Is the starving man stealing food a 'bad' person? Only his actions are unlawful.

The healthier my body and inner life are, the more I can tap into a broader and gentler life view. It has been my purpose to avail myself as much wisdom as my cellular receptors can handle. That means listening and following my intuition. Intuition's referential base abides in a realm of conviction; a perspective of higher purpose and awareness: a faculty rarely open to rational analysis.

For me, treating my body as a temple is the best use of the organic algorithm through which I have the pleasure of experiencing life on this planet.

Human Beings Are Simply...?

Acceptance and surrender are synonymous and are foundational words in the lexicon of awareness. Acceptance implies that a person has laid down the weapons of resistance to their situation. There is a difference between acceptance and resignation. The former is an affirmative action, whereas resignation is a powerless reaction. I want to talk about the role acceptance has played in my life. I accept there is a continuity of life beyond the grave. Concepts such as reincarnation, enlightenment, and multi-dimensional beings were siren calls to my imagination. I gathered all the information I could about these propositions and dispensed it to all who would listen.

I knew that being the dispenser of information was not going to change people's belief systems. The missing ingredient was I had not experienced any of my ideas; they were mind driven concepts. Two years ago, I resolved not to talk authoritatively about scenarios I had not felt in my gut or heart. I want to share my witnessing of four events that qualify me to talk about acceptance, past lives, and other related subjects addressed in these essays.

Aged eighteen, Ian was my best friend. His father was a professional hypnotist. Having watched his father perform and with teenage certainty, he proclaimed his proficiency in the art. My girlfriend, Gloria, was a willing subject and quickly fell into a deep unresponsive trance. After some effort, she responded to the question, *"Do you know your name?"*

"I am Charlotte McDonald."

"Do you know what day it is and where you live?" She replied, *"23rd February 1895."* Scared but curious, we agreed to carry on. She gave her address and told us she was concerned because her grandmother had buried her cat in the garden but would not tell her where.

Enough was enough! It took some time to bring her back into the present. She remembered nothing about the incident. I checked, and yes, the records indicated that a MacDonald family had lived at the address in the 1890s. Did Gloria have a past-life experience? I do not know. But it was proof that we have access to other states of consciousness and timelines.

Irene, in her late 40s, died of cancer after a year-long battle. Her loving partner Joe was overwhelmed, so she asked me to be by her side and support him.

Sitting with her as she moved into a state of acceptance and gratitude was terrific. She was ready to transition into, as she put it, "*a new reality.*" She had preplanned her funeral service and the roles she wanted me and Joe to play. One day, she called me in and said, "*I am ready to go now, please tell Joe and ask if he is ready.*" As she drifted away, I said goodbye with a phrase I used to tease her. "*You're an awful woman.*" Her last words were, "*And you're an awful man.*"

Irene's calm attitude taught me so much about acceptance. When the lifeforce leaves the body, it is an absolute happening. You do not have to be overly sensitive to feel the change in a room. To me, it felt like an entity, an intelligence, had just freed itself from the restrictions of three-dimensional living.

>[1]*The body is nothing but clay without the divine Intelligence permeating it. Divine Intelligence is not only the source of life, it is the reason for it.*

As a young man, I spent many years attempting to ascend and leave the discomfort of being in a body. In retrospect, that was like trying to pilot an aircraft with its sensors and navigation system switched off. Eventually, I started courting myself, becoming a friend, and accepting all these hidden things I had judged. I reconnected, as I now understand it, to the subtleties of my central nervous system. When my essential/child self felt heard and relaxed, my lens of perception changed and is still evolving, allowing for more inclusiveness and compassion to manifest in my life.

Incarnating into this three-dimensional experience is, apparently, in the bucket list of aliens across the galaxy. Given that many of us express a wish to "Go Home," it is ironic that off-planet souls are anxious to incarnate on Earth solely to understand and experience what we are trying to escape from, the friction of duality.

The body is a marvel. Awareness is a gift beyond measure. Following my intuitive directions has brought wisdom and peace into my life.

Peace does not preclude challenges arising; if anything, there are more!

The Potential of Our Children Part 1 of 2

[1]Prior to birth, children have a deep and profound remembrance of dimensional time reference, which preceded the inclusion of clock time. Once children enter this dimension, they are invariably conditioned to function within the frame of reference that their society and parental obligations elicit.

The nature over nurture debate has raged for many centuries. Does the environment or genes determine our behavioral traits? Both play a significant role, but the environment—e.g., parents and childhood imprinting—can overwhelm the child's original genetic blueprint. The ideas presented in the quotes below will likely raise a chorus of detractors. I do not think we are quite ready to give up our sense of owning our kids.

[2]Human parents wish to control their children rather than free them from past constraints. The child's heart and soul are bound up in pleasing the parents rather than developing the core soul matrices that are linked to the "time bites" in his or her awareness.

To a great extent, the circumstances of my family dynamics did allow me to tap into my genetic blueprint. From a young age, I had a strong sense of self with a clear set of values. Bullying and manipulation of the weak and defenseless, whether human or animal, was utterly unacceptable. I felt equal to all and had a strong reaction to the exercise of unbending authority. My adopted parents tried extremely hard to instill their preferences in me while at the same time being dysfunctional in their relationship skills—a case of being unable to practice what they preached. Both passed a long time ago, and I have forgiven them for the traumas I experienced through their dysfunctionality.

Their dysfunctionality afforded me the latitude to develop my thoughts from books rather than parental dogma. I was born as a result of love empowered by the intensity and immediacy of World War II. It was an affair that transgressed social norms and exposed me to a complicated, extraordinary, and beautiful life. I believe I chose to incarnate into that scenario to take charge of a physical temple that was the perfect vehicle to embark on my soul journey through this lifetime.

Many decades into that journey, I can see how the woven patterns of circumstance in my childhood informed many of my erratic behaviors. I was a complete romantic, sold on the fairytale pureness of love portrayed in Doris Day's films.

My first marriage to Vicki, at age twenty, lasted eighteen months. Despite reason screaming, "This is stupid romantic sentimentalism," I went ahead. I was so anxious to be accepted and be in a stable, loving relationship. When the illusional reel of film in my head came to an end, it was very traumatic for us.

Two other marriages crashed before Jungian' Shadow' work, meditation, and deep internal work on self-discipline raised my self-awareness enough to untangle the hooks of childhood trauma at the source of my actions. I can see now that there has been purpose and perfection in all that has happened in my life.

My unconventional upbringing certainly nourished the development of persistence and my sense that there is another trusted hand at the tiller. Somewhere deep in me, I have always known I was looked after and blessed with holding onto part of my pre-birth knowledge.

P.S. Khalil Gibran, the Lebanese poet (1883–1931), had this to say about children: *"Your children are not your children."*

The Potential of Our Children Part 2 of 2

The U.S.A. census in 2012 indicated that 50.5 percent of the seven billion men and women on this planet were under thirty. By 2018, 26 percent of the world population was under fifteen years old. Many of their parents would be millennials born between 1981–1996, are defined as less resilient and more prone to taking offense than previous generations. Intuitively, I feel that they and their progeny create powerful virtual awareness blizzards with effects equivalent in magnitude to the ice ages that reshaped this planet's environment. The rapid advent of communications technology has provided a platform for young, bright new stars with extraordinary talents to enlighten the past's candlelit reality.

In the early 70s, a new breed of highly intelligent empathic children came on the scene, causing upheaval in the education system. Subject to many studies, in 1982, they were named "indigo" children by parapsychologist Nancy Ann Tappe.

Today there are many examples of six to ten-year old's with extraordinary talents. Television and the internet have provided these exceptional children a worldwide stage—for instance, young opera singers with vocal abilities and dispositions well beyond their years. The first was nine-year-old Amira Willeghagen, who in 2013 won the TV show *Holland's Got Talent*. Her voice likened to that of Maria Callas.

Skeptics maintain the view that such genius has always been present. Even if that is the case, it does not detract from the point; it amplifies it; given the opportunity, there are no limits to what we as conscious, self-aware beings can achieve.

In 1994, I struck up a conversation with a woman in a coffee shop in Edinburgh. She was a director of UNICEF (United Nations Children's Fund).

At the time, I was researching Indigo Children and the worrying gap between girls' and boys' educational achievements. Not sure how the concept of Indigos would be received, I gently probed only to discover a very willing and knowledgeable contributor. Here are some of the salient points we covered.

A. *Children see themselves as citizens of the world and are genuinely concerned about the environment.*

B. *Children have developed a sophisticated new computer language that they exclusively use to communicate on the web.*

C. *The intelligence and educational aspirations gap between pre-teen girls and boys is widening. Young men are feeling disenfranchised and turning more toward gangs and violence.*

D. *There was evidence validating the increase in children with extraordinary intellectual powers. She indicated their presence was threatening to parents and teachers. This factor gave rise to the rise in violence, triggering a considerable surge in the use of medication used to counteract their lack of perceived stability. These kids can and do reject standard educational concepts and instructions that make no sense. A kid who can do advanced calculus at age seven will not sit benignly in a math class appropriate for third or fourth graders.*

E. *Young boys feeling threatened psychologically and physically tend to turn toward violence.*

These statements are from 1994. Today in 2020, their predictions turn out to be pretty accurate. The following prophecy is also food for thought.

> [1]*The present state of affairs in the twenty-first century will involve a rapid shift in the calibration of many individuals to a purer uptake of soul data and retrieval of information from other preexistences or future parallel universe information. Therefore, the parent generation will uptake information much more rapidly and will not be strapped with the personality*

characteristics that formulated previous modules. This will allow individuals to become more superfluid in their style of functioning and able to assist others in reaching their full universal potentialities.

Finally, I want to offer some light on the quote below. Unfinished business blocks the development of awareness. In the twentieth century, millions of souls never got half a chance to live a full life. Wars, disease, and genocide have left significant imprints on the psyche of humanity. Whichever deity you choose to nominate as instigator, there was some unfathomable cosmic purpose at play. The timeline of that purpose is unlikely to be clarified in our lifetimes. The upcoming generations hold the key to unlock this puzzle.

[2]During the twentieth century, most individuals did not create a fully developed soul imprint. The souls took on a less progressive character based on a standardized or pooled matrix.

The poem below is worthy of heart-based reflection.

You think of yourself as a citizen of the universe. You think you belong to this world of dust and matter. Out of this dust, you have created a personal image and have forgotten about the essence of your true origin. —RUMi

If your circumstances bring you into contact with autistic children, you will find two inspiring quotes presented in NOTES at the end of the book under the title of this essay.

Developing the Flow of Awareness

As a competitive windsurfer, I spent many hours of training. I relished the fantastic experience of interacting with the wind and the waves. Occasionally, as I sped along in the flow of the waves, the experience was transcendental. There was no "me" as an individual, and no exertion was needed to keep control of the board. I became the wind dancing with the sea and the waves.

A similar event happened in snow skiing. Instead of waves and wind, the stage was powder snow, steepness, and bumps. The impression that remains in my memory was the silence and the sense of just flowing. Exposure to such sensations is not limited to events in the physical realm. All artists touched by an interior connection filling their awareness talk of seeing, feeling, or hearing a sense of Oneness. Ingesting certain substances can produce similar outcomes. I am not judging chemical approaches. Way-showers, often at significant risk, have been needed to push open and embrace new perspectives.

Mainstream thinkers are always ready to challenge the NEW as disruptive. These gatekeepers have successfully held humanity in a fixed, blinkered version of reality necessary to maintain stability until our awareness is ready to herald in a new beginning.

All who read and resonate with this material can play an active role in precipitating the birth of another evolutionary jump, which will push humanity into the dimension of Unity Consciousness.

Every human has within him or her the ability to activate and render our bodies as "dream machines." All that is required is the commitment and willingness to explore the unknown and listen to your inner voice. Commitment's rewards are multifold. Have patience!

The great advantage of following a spiritual path is that the journey is not a linear process. The process, like my windsurfing story, is tidal. For instance, you may have welcomed the unfolding of an amazing revelation only to have it retreat from your consciousness minutes later.

Patience is essential: you have not lost the knowledge; it is not actionable at that time, but it will reappear at the appropriate moment in your timeline.

[1]*The functioning of the body is largely autonomic in scope. The autonomic nervous system is the main component for advanced intelligence in human beings. However, we are not accustomed to thinking that the autonomic nervous system has many advanced stages of symbiotic development.*

"Aha" Moments and Assumptions

I have no doubt that the friction created between what "I" believe and actual reality establishes the conflict that generates my unique life experiences.

The judgment and the influence of my unconscious imprints prevent my nervous system from making decisions based on the moment's needs. My explanations for events and others' behaviors arise from my pre-imprinted presumptions: a need to be right, and my reliance on imperfect memories. Every assumption I have made has always proved to be unfounded.

My "aha" moment occurred at a traffic stoplight. The light turned green, and the car in front remained stationary. I did not honk the horn but felt my blood boil, and my inner critic reveled in creating labels for the vehicle's driver. However, a car I could not see was the problem; it had broken down. My embarrassment was somewhat appeased by helping to push the car to the side shoulder. I vowed afterward to take a breath and repeat. *"Do I know what is going on?... No!... Then breathe."* When I hold to that technique, life's flow is more straightforward, and stress levels drop. The exercise seems to open the door to a new level of empathy and compassion. You can give without loving, but you cannot be loving without giving.

Human beings are creators who look to the future. This impulse to look forward can cause the friction between positivity (a cup half full) and negativity (a cup half empty) approach. When we come to a crossroads, we have choices about the path we take. Suppose we are prone to consider our perception of reality as solely personal and ignore any sense of intuition about possible outcomes. In that case, that self-centric view will, as we step forward, limit our ability to optimize our potential.

In November 2017, my live-in partner and I came to an amicable decision to end our relationship. I was lucky to find a new apartment quickly. By way of celebration, I decided to treat myself to brunch at the top hotel in town. Surprisingly, when I got there, I felt a sense of discomfort. A discomfort that would not diminish. My intuitive voice said, *leave, and have coffee in the local coffee shop.* I followed that inner directive. Feeling at ease, I became immersed in a book. About ten minutes later, I heard a voice close to me say, *"Do you think we have anything to talk about?"* Looking up, I was surprised to see my ex-wife Linda, whom I had not talked to in a couple of years. I said, *"Sit down. Let us find out."* She did, explaining that she had been on her way to the supermarket when she had this strong calling to stop and have a coffee.

Ten months later, we had reached a point where we were discussing renewing our partnership. I felt convinced that the Universe was putting us together to enjoy the sunset of our lives. In November 2018, a medical session revealed Linda had a terminal disease.

I was with her twenty-four hours a day for the seven weeks it took to complete her life cycle. She passed peacefully, in no pain. Her death was quick, peaceful, and almost pain-free, which was a miracle considering tumors were invading her brain. For me, this was a fantastic example of the Universe's compassion. Higher realms called Linda in preparation for another assignment; for that reason, her transition was almost pain-free. A perfect example of second-guessing the Universe, who had other plans! We were, as they say, sailing off to a different kind of sunset.

> [1] *The structure of love and Time is based solely on the experience of the experiencer. The individual grows in his or her relationship to the performance of deeds or situations until he or she is left completely speechless when it comes to understanding the role of the Godforce in the stretching of eternity:*

²The individual is left simply holding the bag of love and is unable to break free from the awe, the wonder of simply viewing life from its raw simplicity and understatedness:

Although that which appears may seem to be as close as the tip of the nose, recognizing what is absolutely right or important is not always so distinctly obvious.

The Body: A Biochemical Marvel

*D*o you have a taste for the latest advances and theories emerging from the quantum scientific community? Can you taste the abstract menu items originating in quantum scientists' communal kitchen: multiverses, wormholes, parallel universes, instant communication between objects light-years apart?

[1]*Human memory must be approached delicately because its internal structure is filled with intelligent ghosts:*

The big question is how humanity can evolve into unity consciousness. First, we have to realign our central nervous system back to its default purpose as a multi-dimensional transmitter/receiver. It appears to be the lead player in how we process and store our memories. The early imprinting of our nervous system creates limitations about how we perceive the world. How do we and the future generations eliminate these dysfunctional impulses frozen in our nervous systems? This is question for each reader to ponder on in the context of your personal contribution to bring balance and peace into your life. Each little shift you make can be equivalent to the analogy of butterfly flapping it's wings: You don't know what a smile might mean to the recipient!

Our memory is full of false flags and is not a dependable source for making personal decisions. When I reflect on how badly I have, in the past, treated my body/nervous system, there are some pretty screwed up memories stored there. These are memories on which I have based actions, then wondered why the efforts did not turn out well. Our bodies are biochemical marvels that require a precise holistic, physical, mental, and spiritual maintenance plan. Most of us treat our cars better than we treat our bodies.

Initiation, Purpose, and Eternity

In 1990, I went to a weeklong retreat held on Sanday, a remote Scottish island. The first couple of days were devoted to grounding me through the application of bodywork treatments. On day three, I took a four-hour walking meditation around the island's rugged coastline. I stepped onto the beach; a sharp north wind was howling encouragement to the enormous waves crashing onto the rocks, causing plumes of foam to fly up the beach. Black heavy clouds were dispassionately observing all this frenetic activity as they sped along, highlighted by a sky's grey backdrop. All my senses came alive. The awe of nature and its ever-changing dynamic focused my attention. All that mattered was staying present in each minute. I watched each great wave crash into impotence in the chaos of the rocks, and I smelled, tasted, and felt the energy of the wave dissipate as it became part of the Oneness of the ocean.

When I returned to the center, the two healers/psychics facilitating the retreat were waiting. They looked at me for a moment, exchanged a few words, then asked me to change and meet them in the workroom. The ambiance, warmth, and the soft earth-colored patterned drapes enveloped me, and I felt safe. I lay down on the massage table, and they covered me in a woolen blanket. I was in a secure womblike bubble. They gently told me their guides had sought and received my higher self's permission to access my akashic records. According to these records, the session was startling and revealing; my mission in this lifetime is to research across the whole breadth of spiritual endeavors to accumulate information and experience. Do this because, in some later time, people with many questions will seek the wisdom of knowing emanating from you. We are not permitted to tell you from which galaxy you came. We can say, presently, there are only four others from the same source incarnated on this planet.

I had a mission that filled me with a deep sense of well-being and a new sense of self. Part of my journey was surrendering to the truth and reality of my existence. Ego is a fantastic servant but a terrible master. I needed to harness my ego, not throw it out with the bathwater.

We are eternal beings serving in a non-eternal role. Embracing our Oneness will facilitate the flowering of our developing, infinite abilities.

[1]*As sentient life is essentially free, it is also essentially eternal. It only pictures itself as noneternal for the purposes of the experiment. Sentient life has an eternal aspect, but it does not identify with this aspect, for the purpose of learning and growth:*

The last quote contains an amazing and beautiful statement about the infinite longing of the Godhead. The message resonates, like the waves on Sanday, I can taste, smell, and feel my individuality dissipating as I become part of the Oneness.

[2]*Filled with longing for infinite knowing and stretched further than the boundaries the human mind can travel, God relates the experience of time to His own understanding, and develops time through the continuity of civilizations and hegemonies that form the backdrop for a sentient world:*

The Dynamics of Sentience

Here are some fundamental questions for your consideration. Why has pain and wretchedness caused by the existence of opposite polarities been inflicted on humanity? Why is there a system of constraints that impose the layering of the imprints in our psyche?

Most of our actions and thoughts are repetitive, circular reflections of the past or an imagined future. "Action speaks louder than words" is a cliché; we tend not to place much value on subjective assessment, so our judgments can lack balance—people whose life choices based on past experiences tend not to step out of their routine parameters. The most challenging assumption to step away from is that we are the originators of what we think and feel.

The impulses that power our thought processes are set in motion by permanent imprints veiled from our awareness. It is not easy to give credence to the fact that many of our actions have no basis or are even relevant to the present's actual needs. Here is a simple example of behavior not based on the needs of the present moment.

In the UK, I drove right-hand drive cars for thirty years. However, even after going on the left for the last twenty-two years, I still absentmindedly reach up with my left hand to grab the seat belt—embarrassing and potentially dangerous. Initially, driving on the left was stressful; in one instance, I found myself pulling into the oncoming traffic flow. That incident was a wake-up call. However, any relaxation of awareness, like being tired, distracted, or stressed, can lead to the old default straining at the leash to take over. In situations such as this, becoming fully conscious and present is vital.

In closing, I have deep compassion for those tied to beliefs installed by religions that preach humans are inherently sinners. They have to seek absolution by a God that, through a priesthood, delivers punishment for one's sins by condemning one's soul to HELL! Such outlooks have shrunk the hearts of their congregations and buried their empathy for diversity. I respect their right to believe, but when these believers try to impose their dogma on others, the friction of positive and negative turns into conflict.

At this time of transition, we are fortunate to have all the information needed to transcend and evolve into Unity consciousness. The speed of change in the world beckons us to re-evaluate every fixed idea to adapt and participate consciously in this evolutionary process.

Factors of Human Personality

Our personality traits play a significant role in determining how we each face the experiences of life. Personality type determines how we deal with existential problems and how we process our responses to physical and psychological events.

There are three basic personality types. The attributes and the limitations they access to make sense of life's challenges are listed below. While you should be able to identify your dominant trait, you will more than likely share aspects from all the others. In the eyes of the Divine, all types are of equal importance in the game of life. My essential self has a longing for the secure foothold in life that personality type one enjoys. Predominantly, I am type three. These descriptions may seem like a labeling exercise that immediately raises a red flag in essays stressing Oneness. The aim is not to label people, but through knowledge, accept their journey through life and make your decisions from that broad standpoint.

> [1]*Fluid Individuals are apt to fall down when reconciling their psychological and highly personal needs with the event structure as a whole. They are not capable of holding their own when a certain set of parameters presents itself. These individuals have a tendency to lose themselves in what is presented to them. However, because they are so malleable, they are also able to see what is presenting itself is the same thing in many different guises. This perceptual understanding gives them the ability to see behind event structures.*

I interpret this example as a person who cannot control her or his boundaries, which is a cross many empaths carry. Influences from different psychological realms compete for dominance and cause stress. Their wisdom arises from their perceptual understanding and is available to those who listen with sensitivity and patience.

> [2]The more fixed or rigid personality has a difficult time seeing that what he or she is perceiving is purely a symbolic construct of his or her individual reality. He or she must see reality as a rigid, fixed form for the sake of security and individuality. By seeing oneself as drawn into a finite continuum of possible outcomes, one feels a sense of freedom in that there are limited possibilities for either success or failure. One has a secure foothold on life that causes a pure feeling of individuation free from contamination by outside forces.

I call this personality type a gatekeeper. At an early age, I learned how consequential these types are. I have always known that power comes hand in hand with the person who holds the keys to their level. When I was late, the school janitor unlocked the gate and let me in; or could, against the rules, open the lost property cupboard to choose an item I needed.

Gatekeepers are prevalent on every level of institutions, including spiritual gates. They appear to be rigid; however, the way to open their 'gate' is to listen doing so validates their individuation intently.

> [3]These beings freed from either stance, not dependent on the event streams confronting them are unbound by temporal demands. They live through cognizing their own gravitational center at every moment. This condition referred to as liberation, simply frees up the ground under which the individual walks. It is not a determination of worth or stature in God's eyes, nor does it make him or her exempt from the "taxes" extracted by karma. It simply allows the individual to stand in a place where the event structures no longer perfectly mirror the psychological consciousness.

My type is recognizable by their directness. We tend to be non-respecters of the 'sanctity' of the mainstream mindset. Another clue is their light-heartedness and ability to laugh at the challenge. They may also be athletic, insofar as they take care of their bodies, and one can almost see or feel that they have anchored the light into their physical form. I have some glitches, impatience, and little sympathy for procrastination.

Identity, attachment is a distinct and ubiquitous aspect of our personalities, which as the perpetrator, I find amusing, and conversely, self-righteous indignation when I am the victim. A blatant example of this behavior showed up when we were on a beach vacation in the Mediterranean. No matter what time of day, every deck chair at the swimming pool had towels hanging on them—a clear signal of ownership. Frustrated, we got up predawn only to find towels already laid out. Enough was enough! We took every towel off the chairs and placed them in a bundle beside the diving board. By 8:30 a.m., anarchy had broken out; couples were fighting, claiming that the seated parties had taken their places. It was the most satisfying comedy theater. When I walk into the coffee shop to find my seat by the window occupied in my victim role, I glare at the occupants. "Don't they know that's my seat or my parking place?" As humans, we measure our identity and self-worth by what we own, be it material wealth or a strong sense of victimhood, which we tenaciously wear on our sleeve.

Identity attachment has its roots in fear and is the cockroach aspect of all humanities' quirks! No matter how hard we try, it is impossible to eliminate it. Anxiety, the loss of identity, and self-worth played a dominant role in the unfolding of this personal drama. As a young man, I loved camping and took every opportunity to do so on the beach or in Scotland's mountains. Yet four decades later, when my wife, a keen adventurer, wanted to go camping in Mexico's Baja wilderness, I resisted; my imagination conjured up unpleasant scenarios. My stance caused her great disappointment.

When I eventually dug the reason for the fear out of my subconscious, its roots were imprints from early youth. The only knowledge I had of

Mexican culture was through exposure to Western movies—movies in which Mexicans were thieves and murderers. Acting out on these fearful impressions in front of Linda severely limited our ability to share a deeper relationship. I was so frightened that admitting my fear would blow my identity as a streetwise man. Instead, it blew my wife's respect for me out the window.

We are all part of the ONE. Our individual experiences add to the whole, even if how they do so is alien to our sensibilities. I honor the fact that everyone's life journey is as it needs to be. We are the architects of our experiences, whether or not we acknowledge it. Undoubtedly, external events impinge, but we retain control of how we react to them. Our actions and reactions are the directional footsteps of our journey.

In the jigsaw of existence, every piece plays an equal part in constructing the big picture.

Patience: The lifeblood of Beauty and Order.

Most spiritual practices emphasize not to try to attain enlightenment because trying is a function of the ego. Wisdom arises through surrender, hard work, and meditation, the goal being to subdue the ego. *"Have patience"* is the advice delivered to disciples when their frustration comes to the surface.

> [1]*To arrive at this state, it is necessary to become extremely patient. This is true because patience, in relationship to time, is the supreme virtue.*

There is such depth of meaning behind the word patience. I will make a bold statement. When you achieve a continuous state of patience, you reach a stage of Enlightenment. Yet, you will still feel the pain of injustice.

In our daily lives, the subject of the lack of patience arises as a reaction to incompletion. I am sure you can think of many examples when the conflict between expectations and reality tests your ability to cut yourself some slack and recognize there is more than one way to achieve something? In hindsight, we usually beat ourselves up about our impatience. We judge ourselves for not being loving, not being kind, and being wrong. We get swallowed in a cornucopia of heavy self-deprecation.

The more absorbed we become in self-judgments, the more substantial and painful these self-judgments become. Why? Prescription asserts that this kind of self-flagellation is the only way to improve yourself. Following any dogma means overriding our authentic self and becoming hemmed in by a lack of openness, freedom, and self-respect.

Such practices are the benchmark of old paradigm mainstream religious teachings. A child lovingly encouraged to seek out his or her path and grow up with the ability to extend love, e.g., patience in all matters, will have a perspective that allows them to handle all injustices as part of the big picture and have little meaning.

Being aligned does not make dealing with daily life any more comfortable or exempt me from the consequences of living in a three-dimensional reality. However, I can live in greater harmony with the Universe, which, in turn, allows me to seize each moment as an opportunity for growth and heart-centered consciousness.

As a teenager, I enjoyed experimenting with out-of-body experiences. I could sidestep the travails of human life. There is no denying that such short-lived experiences could be exquisite. Now, being fully anchored in the temple of my body brings much joy.

When I let patience blossom without concern about meeting some goals, I am free to complete the moment's need

Awakening the Language of Awareness

[1]Civilization has become accustomed to excising individuals and cultures that do not ascribe to the type of linguistic mores that its situation demands. Since individuals are unable to develop their own highly specialized and unique forms of communication, the collective interpretation of reality has become the rule.

For thousands of years, humanity led a peaceful nomadic life moving with the seasons that determined their food supply. There is no real evidence of serious conflict between the diverse groups. Hardly surprising because conflict triggers like land ownership of water, and food was nonexistent. Earth's plentitude was a bounty for all to share. So, what changed? The climate!

The ice ages and droughts eventually forced people to cluster in one place for their survival and heralded in civilization's birth as we know it. Boundaries and ownership allowed for the consolidation of power by groups with specific agendas, such as the priesthood. My pet theory about God's "Tower of Babel" punishment is that people were displaying pride and arrogance by wanting to be like him. Because of this impertinence, he decided to fragment the peoples' everyday language. Perhaps the story was constructed by a human observer as a metaphor depicting the power struggle between the free will of the individual and the priesthood's brutal power.

In the childhood of civilization, where rules ensure survival, there is a good argument for cooperative collective systems. However, there also comes a time when the baby, collectively and individually, must grow up.

Humanity is now at that point. The graduation into personal responsibility for the good of the whole is a prerogative—a prerogative fueled by heart-centered processes, powered by an advanced multi-dimensional language. I want to share an example of the draconian use of power, unleashed by breaking some language taboos.

At the age of ten, I arrived home from school, proud and anxious to share, with my mother, the poem I had just learned in the playground.

> *My brother lies over the ocean.*
>
> *My sister lies over the sea.*
>
> *My father lies over my mother,*
>
> *and that is how my mother got me.*

The blur of her hand was the last thing I saw before a blinding pain smashed through my body. She screamed, "Wicked, sinful, wicked boy," dragged me to my bedroom. Many years later, I understood what the poem meant.

Power used indiscriminately to prop up some belief happens across the whole spectrum of human behavior ad nauseam. As individuals, we all have the opportunity to stop reacting from old habits and beliefs. For example, how much awareness would it have taken for her to realize I had no idea what I was talking about and exercise constraint? I forgave my mother a long time ago.

> [2]*Time is the balance beam on which consciousness places itself. It is up to language to correct the forward or backward movement that is naturally created when time impulses feed themselves directly into the nervous system. Sometimes this may be seen as a type a quivering of articulation of the individual as the proper sequestration lines up in the cerebrospinal cortex for germination and expression.*

A complex way to say, words are enormously powerful. Choose them wisely, and you will feel the energy behind these words surge through your body.

The Present Borrows from
the Past and Future.

The stress of ambivalence is a familiar occurrence in our daily lives. Our nature ensures our minds remain attuned to the past and future. We turn to the past for inspirational crumbs that will inform and resolve present dilemmas. At the same time, we are prone to throwing future predictions into the mix. Relying on these ingredients can lead to decisions that further down the path will make no sense. Hardly surprising! Our memories are full of emotionally charged energies that can influence our behavior without conscious knowledge; I call these occurrences the 'Blue Room' effect.

I was one of two candidates for a high-level post. When I met the panel, the predominantly blue décor theme of the room impacted me. I felt uncharacteristically nervous, which intensified as the interview progressed. I emerged having failed to impress the panel—most of my answers were ambivalent and indecisive.

Years later, in therapy, I unwrapped a traumatic experience of abuse, which had taken place in a room where all four walls were painted blue. The blueness of the interview room had triggered a robust cellular response in me.

We gather our predictive input from interesting stories we invent. These Stories give meaning to our predictive process despite their lack of basis in reality.

How would I deal with the blue room effect now? Deep belly breathing and silently chant my mantra. Failing that, I would ask to be excused for a minute and regroup in the restroom.

Our ability to access the past and the future is hard-wired. As my self-awareness evolves, I still borrow from both timelines. The more present I am, the more "Light" is available to see and hear the subtle information and intuitions that emanate from past and future possibilities. Like when for no reason, you slow down more than usual on the blind corner only to meet an oncoming vehicle halfway into your lane.

Anyone close to me would readily agree that I am rarely fully present, as they would put it. As a teenager, adults identified this lack of attention as arrogance. I could readily jump from past to future; both places were more interesting than the present. In the late nineteen fifties, I was fascinated with books depicting the 21st century. Now that the future is here, while many predictions never came to fruition, many others have accelerated beyond expected timelines.

The rhythms of life that once took centuries to change now do so in months, if not weeks—a destabilizing scenario for many folks. We swim in the sea of illusion with little regard for the needs of other sentient beings. We are currently in the middle of a rapidly evolving situation: one that shows that the whole human community needs should be considered a priority.

The Godforce has granted us tremendous latitude about how long we dally in the ocean of individuality. However, stasis is not the preferred dynamic of the Godforce!

Words and actions have consequences beyond our local sphere, eluded in the analogy‥ ‡‡ *The air from a butterfly's wings can cause a hurricane in another location.* We need to wield the power of our actions and words with care. Time's hand is on the tiller of our journey through the ocean of experience. I urge you to approach all events with love and compassion for all beings; doing so will ensure the needs of "the Whole" be fulfilled with minimum disruption.

---

‡‡   The Chaos Theory: a phenomenon named by mathematician James A. Yorke in 1975.

The outcome is up to each individual. The words and actions of an individual in the present have a great deal to do with what event streams will become available in the future.

In other words, wisdom is there for all who care to look.

The Limits of the Ego

O ne of Ego's core functions is to ensure the survival of the body. The Ego also provides the power of passion, which drives our imagination and creativity. However, without oversight, the Ego is left to do what it thinks best for our survival. the Ego's desires have threatened instead of enhancing humanity's survival!

On a personal note, my horrendous divorce was the proving ground for my ability to remain neutral and withstand the onslaught of a distraught ego. How can one resist the vicious abuse claiming the high ground of being the "betrayed" one? And at the same time, manage the rampaging inner howl of my Ego screaming *abandoned, not understood,* and needing revenge?

My resolve to practice neutrality was "fine and dandy" until someone I loved started asking questions loaded with innuendo and designed solely to validate their point of view. Our exchanges came to a breaking point when I was accused of doing something I did not do, and I lost it. Metaphorically, that is when my trigger finger pulled hard, though, in retrospect, the frustration at hearing the same accusations, again and again, had already caused finger tension. My storyline says I am always accurate and speak from a truthful place! Not true! So, when faced with the accusation, my suppressed denial had been called out, despite the fact, in this example, I was in a "cry wolf" situation. I learned four things from that incident:

1. There are always levels upon levels to uncover from the unconscious mind.

2. I should be grateful and hold the reins softly even when the unexpected pops up.

3. Any idea I hold sacrosanct needs more in-depth scrutiny.

4. Never change anyone's spiritual beliefs unless you are confident you can replace them with a higher truth. Because if you change a person's beliefs, you take on the karma created by that action.

    "There is an unexplored role that the ego plays, which ultimately leads to greater spiritual progress. The Ego is an essential factor in bringing us deeper Self-knowledge."—ACHARYA SHUNYA.

    I am genuinely committed to welcoming the softness of the heart.

Becoming a Multi-dimensional Being

To describe the indescribable is not possible. What I see is an inner vision depicting "a timeless knowing" on an inner canvas. A canvas capable of expressing all senses as a spontaneous gallery of multi-dimensional, infinite possibilities—just being in the flow!

Being in the flow is an easy answer to describe an indescribable experience. Sportsmen and women who achieve the extraordinary tend to use flow to describe the indescribable. The experience is not exclusive to active sports. However, because their remarkable results are usually publicly witnessed, they often face questions by an excited media demanding to know how they did it.

One flow event stands out; it occurred during a windsurfing competition. Fifteen competitors huddled on the beach, the wind buffering and blustering, exciting both foam and sand into aerial combat with our bodies. We were braced, ready to challenge the almost mocking fierce blasts, creating wave sets with flecks of foam springing from their lips. These conditions focus the mind; the *price of bread is of no consequence at moments like that!*

The start gun barked, and we were off, blasting toward the gybe point back to the inshore marker buoy. On the second run out, I was in the leading three. It was in that instant that time stopped. The battle with the wind and waves became a graceful ballet. There was no separation between me, the board, the sail, and the sea.

In perfect synchronicity, as a single unit in complete cooperation, I made the last turn, and the experience ended just as suddenly as it had started.

The big difference between "flow" and my ordinary awareness was that my doubts, fears, and uncertainties about my ability to navigate heavy seas no longer existed.

As I recall this event, I felt as though I was looking through a kaleidoscope. Colored waves of energy weaved and danced around me in a slow spiral. Most of all, I remember being enclosed in a bubble of peace.

Blissful states of meditation have produced similar experiences. The only difference is my body in meditation is static. In comparison, my body was fully involved in the real adventure—fully alive, with all energy centers firing. Dervishes and Shakers use their bodies to induce transcendent states. In these rituals, the concerns of the body and mind surrender.

Perhaps the same happens when in the moments of deepest psychological and physiological despair, the hand of revelation reaches out. You emerge from the long 'dark' night of the soul.

A Game-changing Gift

In the essay "The Limits of the Ego,*" I stated that my horrendous divorce was the proving ground for my ability to remain neutral and withstand the onslaught of a distraught ego. There were other consequences; a heart emotionally and physically was broken. A gifted healer and friend stepped out of protocol to warn me that the divorce trauma was placing a tremendous strain on my heart, and unless I came to a place of inner calmness, I was in danger of dying. Two years later, in 2016, that dire prophesy started to unfold. I underwent open-heart surgery. The experience was a game-changing gift that I want to share through the eyes of my spiritual awareness.

I was playing an exhibition table tennis match when my pulse started to beat unusually. The healer's warning flashed before my eyes. I immediately drove to the emergency room, and I am thankful for that moment of decision.

From day one, I felt surrounded by angels in human form. I felt embraced by love and goodwill, and intuitively, there were many other guides from other dimensions in constant attendance. All my life, I have felt supported in many realms. While consulting with the surgeon, we discovered we had a mutual friend, a table tennis buddy of mine. The son of another friend, an anesthesiologist, volunteered to be on duty for my operation. He introduced himself beforehand. It was a great comfort to know I had two people in the operating theater who knew me. When I regained consciousness, Grace, my then partner, was standing at my bed's foot engaged in some hands-off healing work. Gratitude flooded through me. Throughout my time in the hospital, Grace was able to bring all her intuitive healing and guidance into play. The week before this event, she complained that her schedule for the following weeks was uncharacteristically empty (now we knew why). Bless her, it was not an easy time for her.

Two other dear friends gave 100 percent of their energy and love for our well-being. They held us in a vast green bubble of heart healing love. I also want to acknowledge two of the charge nurses (angels) in Mission's Heart tower who chose to be my advocate and individual caregivers. I truly felt held in healing hands.

The surgeon told me later that on a recovery scale of 1 to 10, I was a 10. Every medical professional who worked with me expressed amazement at my speed and ease of recovery. I felt I had received a great gift.

In the months that followed, I felt like a newborn; my physical heart renewed—this was the gift of a second chance.

Eight years previous, a tarot reader told me in astonishment, "I have never met anyone who chose to live two lives in one incarnation. Usually, people transition and are reborn, but you have chosen to go through this rebirth in the same body. You will need courage because some of the changes will, on the surface, be devastating. You have an important mission on this planet, but you will have to realign your body and consciousness to allow the energies and knowledge to sit within you without frying you. Good luck."

I find it challenging to come to terms with the fact that I had a significant operation purely because my experience was so easy, so seamless, so pain-free, and so full of loving support. I emphasize again that I am sure that my sixty years of spiritual curiosity and research equipped me to deal with all this.

I have come to accept that in the "big picture," everything is as it should be despite the fear and anger lurking in my consciousness's hidden corners. I have learned to love and accept that all these parts of me needed love, not rejection.

"Love is the only sane and satisfactory answer to the problem of human existence." Erich Fromm. German psychologist (1900–1980). Fromm also proposed that love is more than a warm and fuzzy feeling in our hearts.

"It's a creative force that fuels our willpower and unlocks hidden resources."

Transformation: Human Potential

Looking or just touching the fruits growing in the grove of spirituality robs you of having a full experience. You can hold a peach and pass on information about its color and form. But only when you take a bite can you genuinely claim you had a full personal experience with the peach.

Like the above example, rarely, if ever, does the strong urge to follow ego-based reviews have any connection to the reality of the present moment. I cannot stress enough to dive deep if you want to walk clear and taste the fruits of the present moment.

The struggle between mental concepts and intuitive knowing can create cognitive dissonance. The personality needs to be right. Intuition demands acceptance of what is. In the past, I never questioned the nature and scope of my success. I did lament failures, always identifying an outside factor as the nemesis of my project. That bias reflected my need to be right. I have since learned that the sense of completeness that follows intuitive action does not need to be confirmed or shouted from the rooftops. The learning has been to thank the ego for its contribution, then sit quietly and listen for the subtle tones of intuition, the mouthpiece of reality.

If we move in the presence of reality rather than inventing little parables to motivate ourselves, reality becomes simultaneous and instantaneous. However, I cannot speak to that depth of engagement, but in a way, I am describing the innocence of a child playing entirely in the present moment.

As a child, I lived in Edinburgh. Mrs. Talland, my primary school teacher, had traveled extensively in Africa. She captivated the class with stories from that continent and tales of mysteries imprinted in the old Edinburgh fabric. Another stimulant was the Rupert Bear annual, which came down the chimney every Christmas full of stories about magicians and magic creatures.

The images and words seeped into my awareness, fueling a lifelong interest in the extraordinary.

I came across poetry, written some forty years ago. As I read, I thought, *did I write this stuff?* It seemed I had tapped into a source of timeless, rich inner experiences.

A step beyond language

Step through the forest on a silent retreat.

Realign your soul to the impulse of the Divine.

There, in the majesty of Natures courtyard, sense the Oneness

in which you are entwined.

Open your heart to the loving tapestry all around.

Every aspect of you is woven into this design, by the thread of creation

in which you are entwined.

In the silence, broken only by the crack of a twig,

you hear the subtle sound of the engine of love.

A sound that strikes language from your lips,

and confirms the Divine relationship,

in which we are entwined.

Just Listen:

Be patient. You do not need others to confirm your truth.

Those that want to know are drawn to you.

They will recognize what they are seeking,

so, be there and listen.

Watch how a person glows when you listen.

Listening is the ultimate salute to the sovereignty of the speaker. Intuition contains the wisdom we need to achieve the state of multi-dimensional beingness. There is no question, my life flow is calmer, and relationships are more profound when I accept it is what it is as the bedrock of my existence. I encourage you to taste life as a fruit, sometimes bitter, sometimes sweet, but ultimately nourishing your learning about the connection between all the "orchard fruits" abiding on Earth.

Celestial Plans Are Infinitely Variable

Loch Lomond in Scotland is well-known as a beautiful tourist destination. However, the deep waters of the loch harbor unseen dangers. Underwater ledges trap, then release frigid water carried in strong currents; this danger is well signposted!

One hot day long ago, I went swimming in the loch. The water was freezing, but as my friends admired me for doing so, I plunged on. Suddenly, I felt like my legs were becoming ice-cold, and I was losing feeling in them. Panicking, I struck out for the shore. I was lucky I made it, but my legs from the knee down were grey white. As I said, this danger is well signposted. Like me, motivated by ego, people think they know better and ignore the signs: an occurrence that mirrors our ignorance of the danger signs prominently posted by the planet.

With blinders firmly fitted to our eyes, we stubbornly strive to maintain our tribal identities, firmly convinced that we will be unsupported and alone if we do not. This deeply embedded belief distorts our veiled memories of leaving the realm of "Soul Unity" to explore this material world. Memories that give us the impression we were expelled from "paradise," when in truth, we chose to incarnate here. We deliberately veiled our mind ensuring full commitment to experiencing the rights and wrongs, the good and evil, that is the dance of opposites necessary to enhance life's learning on this planet.

Despite humanity's apparent addiction to childish whims, the Divine, I suspect, relishes this creation for the extraordinary challenges humanity has produced, which unwittingly creates new variables in the algorithm of "Time." We keep the Lords of Time fully occupied in tweaking that algorithm to account for these variables. Humanity is playing in the Gods' playground, not as an active partner as envisioned in the grand plan, but as delinquent children capable of destruction on a large scale. It is well that the Divine has infinite patience.

While destruction on a large scale is a possible fate of Mankind, celestial plans are infinitely adaptable. How do I know that? I do not know! Let me invite you to open your imagination and step into an inner space where such thoughts and references have a context. Let us start with this quote.

> [1]*Mankind is a multitemporal, multispatial race, built upon many seed races that have been stocked here over millennia. We are, therefore, neither fully human nor fully divine, but a kind of crossbred configurations of beings.*

The statement about humans being the product of many seed races might be problematic for those who believe we are the only species in God's kingdom.

Tom Kenyon[*§§] speaks of the involvement of seed races. I will paraphrase. *Before humanity's "die was cast," there had been over twenty attempts at genetic tampering from different alien civilizations. Because we have such a mélange of gene information, we are considered intergalactic royalty.*

My genes might qualify for royal status, but that has not stopped life's whims from occasionally launching me into the rough sea of doubt, a voyage that is anything but smooth. I cherish my intuition and strive to stay receptive to its subtle and sometimes seemingly conflicting messages.

In this time of fluidity and uncertainty, I can no longer rely on my old inner reference library to find stability. Nothing is where it used to be in my internal card index. A small tornado of change funneled its way through the door of my perception bearing the gift of chaos to the filing system. However, I receive more than enough indications from my guides to trust that intuition is navigating.

---

§§   Tom Kenyon, MA & Judy Sion: *The Arcturian Anthology* 2013. ISBN #978-1-931032-46-9

Male and Female: The Universal Mystery!

We have within us both masculine and feminine aspects. Each of us faces the problem of reconciling and balancing these conflicting approaches: the male conceptual, mental, and sharp approach, and the slower, tender, and heart-based process of the feminine. We tend to adopt a gender-based stand on issues. In conflict, we look outside ourselves to attribute blame for our failure to resolve issues. This factor is a mirror reflecting the battle that is raging just below our awareness. But as the quotes below suggest, the male/female dilemma emanates from a UNIVERSAL mystery.

> [1]One cannot say how the concepts of male and female have been developed. This universal mystery, connected to celestial intelligence, appears to be essentially arbitrary.

> [2]The flow of creation toward the feminine is a slower, more gracefully timed determination. The flow toward the masculine is quicker, more expedient, direct, and sharp. When celestial intelligence is in the process of determining the sex of a creature, a clearly delineated choice is not always made ahead of time.

The point which stands out is the assertion regarding the determination of a creature's sex being open to chance because "delineated choice is not always made ahead of time." That statement epitomizes the purpose of creation. A mission, powered by the engines of contrast and friction, crafted to allow the potentialities of life, love, compassion, acceptance, patience, and creation to be fully expressed. The quote also consolidates the significant role the Divine Mother plays across the full spectrum of Nature.

Humanity, especially all beings who espouse the distortions of male dominance, needs to respect the Mother (if we want to survive). There are some limitations that we need to address. We need to harmonize the substantial cultural gaps that create the patriarchal elite and end the crisis caused by male/female pursuit before we can step into full partnership with other sentient beings in the universe.

These inner conflicts are the core of all human disunity. We are predisposed to mirror our groups' negative aspects (The Golem effect) and imitate the positive elements (The Pygmalion effect).

The first step toward inner balance is to look inside and rescue our courage; then, we can stand firm and deal with our limitations. They are responsible for destabilizing our ability to interact as loving, compassionate beings—humanity's God-given birthright.

The Liquidity of Awareness

When we use our body, mind, and heart as a conduit to the Oneness of the Divine, we gain access to the fruit offered from the vine of life. A fruit that enhances broadens and opens our awareness to the multi-faceted tools at our disposal.

These divine offerings are not prescriptive, nor is any judgment delivered to how an individual chooses to receive these fruits. Each being's journey is unique and equally important, regardless of how it plays out in our right/wrong social environment. Society, though, needs guidelines that encourage personal accountability for our actions.

Many years ago, I had a friend who was a competitive middle-distance runner—being Type A personality, he treated his body like a machine, there to do his bidding. He complained about having to drink water during a race to stay hydrated. He argued that if the body needed so much water, why does it quickly need to relieve itself? He devised a protocol to control the peristalsis process. He told his body to *shut up*. Now, in his elder years, he has severe bowel and intestinal problems.

I do not judge him because I have no access to his soul purpose. But his attitude is a perfect example of disregard for the body, which he treated as a compliant servant. It is all a matter of perspective and the avenues of response we choose to thread through in our lifetime.

The following wisdom from *The Recognition Sutras* by Christopher Wallis*⁋⁋ offers direction for those who choose to treat the body as a temple where consciousness temporally resides.

⁋⁋   *The Recognition Sutras* by Christopher Wallis 2017 ISBN #978-0-987613-9-0

Stilling the mind's storytelling and cultivating contacts with precursive reality. Place your mind in your heart. The heart is the synonym for awareness, so entrust the mind to the heart. It's simply bringing reverent attention to awareness itself. The term awareness includes not only all that is but all that could be. So, the field of awareness feels full of all the phenomena one perceives and yet has room for more. We are then encouraged to think of nothing, and this can be achieved by becoming disinterested in the content of thought.

Wisdom teachings have standard threads but are often hard to correlate because they can be the subtext of the content. In this instance, I do not think you will have a problem appreciating the connection between the quote below and the one before it, stated by Wallis.

> [1]*The individual arrives at a state of awareness in which the choices or liquidities that are available in the awareness are capable of unifying completely. This state involves a complete change in the orientation of the individual from masking awareness to formulating awareness.*

A phrase from Wallis's quote stands out for me.

We are then encouraged to think of nothing, and this can be achieved by becoming disinterested in the content of thought.

My thoughts, which I used to believe were vitally important to my well-being, no longer overwhelm me with emotional reaction, though they still vie for attention.

Strategies of the Divine Plan

"Hope in reality is the worst of all evils because it prolongs the torment of men." —F. NIETZSCHE

Nietzsche[***] was adamant. We should not believe in anything we cannot know. I propose that our torment comes from trying to understand and analyze consciousness solely from a cerebral perspective. When faced with the mysterious, the heart has to be engaged to access genuine knowingness, which is an axiom beyond words and understanding.

I love sitting in the hot tub, sauna, and steam room of the local YMCA. I occasionally re-read the rules applicable to the facility's use: Nobody under 16 years of age—the recommended time in each unit 10 to 15 mins. No glassware. No outdoor shoes. Shower before entering the pool. All prominently displayed to achieve a goal: safety. Some individuals challenge or ignore the notices but, when confronted, profess Ignorance, resulting in drama as they project their emotions onto the challenger.

An ancient proverb states, Ignorance of the law is no excuse. But we humans exercise our Ignorance in many ways and often expect to escape the consequences. Let us transform this local drama onto a hypothetical celestial stage. In this big picture script.

[1]Celestial objects are inherently selfless in that they serve the intelligent civilizations in their influence without pause. On the other hand, they are selfish in the sense that they look toward their own development first and will throw off those civilizations

---

[***] Frederick Nietzsche: (1844–1900) German philosopher had a profound influence on modern intellectual history.

or cultural influences that will directly retard their self-determination.

What if humanity does not come up to scratch and is, with permission from Mother Intelligence, thrown off by Gaia? Imagine the wailing and gnashing of teeth and shouts of protest about the injustice; we *did not know and had no warning!* In this case, ignorance of the law would not be a valid excuse. Throughout the ages, predictions about the rules governing incarnation on Earth have been handed down by every spiritual means of communication. *Strive for peace, cooperation, compassion, love, and come to know that all sentient beings are an equal part of the ONE.*

The quote below might appear elitist, but it upends our notion about autonomy, free will, and our place at the center of things.

[2]*As the universe matures, it is the Mother intelligence that directs the formation of sentience and determines the degree to which it will become functionally participant in the intelligent life of that sector.*

From the moment we discovered language, love has been the most positive bonding experience shared by all humans. Yet, every day we are bombarded by words of negativity and horrors we inflict on each other. How, in this pressure cooker, do we establish balance? Love can turn on the taps of ecstasy or despair. The friction between these two emotions is the base narrative of every human drama story ever told.

George Monbiot, a: British author and environmental and political activist, argues for the need to create a new narrative for living that will awaken the attributes of altruism and cooperation in every human's heart. We all experience love: love of family, love of our community, love of fellow creatures. We all have the urge to help the innocent, the weak, and the sick. How would we make these attributes go viral? How do we create this new narrative for "living"? Maybe I will not have to jump in front of a vehicle to save a child. But I can greet everyone with respect as part of my global family.

We all operate in various degrees of consciousness, yet we are all equal in our dependence on Mother Earth. Our contributions are significant when distilled into information necessary for our survival and evolution. The universe is composed of civilizations of various degrees of conscious uniformity and order. There are no lesser or greater life forms.

The extract below from Carter Phipps's*††† book *Evolutionaries* highlights the perspective about how significant and extraordinary our evolution is, and how amazing we can be; how gifted we are to have "God-given" sentience.

> *From the dust 5 billion years ago, we have evolved and will continue to do so because that is just the nature of humans; things change. Today we can choose to direct our destiny. No longer must we stumble through this event called human life with little sense of whence we came, clinging with closed eyes, to ancient myths or outdated world-views, staggering from crisis to crisis, reacting as best we can to the news of the day.*
>
> *But little by little, we have opened our eyes and started to glimpse the enormity of the picture. We should not underestimate the import of our moment in this history after eons of blind, unconscious evolution; a creature exists who can decide consciously to evolve.*

I am sure many of you have toyed with the hope that this is your last incarnation, and you will then reside forever in some heaven or think death is the END! In the Divine's timeless presence, the passing of eons and millions of years is just a "time-bound" linear illusion that does not exist in Divine reality. We are, whether we like it or not, spiritual beings, no exceptions. We all equally serve the divine purpose.

---

††† Carter Phipps is a best-selling author of *Evolutionaries* (Harper Perennial 2012). He is co-founder of the Institute for Cultural Evolution.

As we discuss cosmic perspectives, I want to acknowledge the discomfort experienced by those who, like me, struggle to come to terms with a deep inner conviction that your origins were not on this planet.

From the book *The Arcturian Anthology* by Tom Kenyon and Judi Sion, I offer this transmission from Mary Magdalen speaking as an Arcturian who embodied as a human being.

As a human woman, I understand the needs of the heart.

The pressure of being human and an emanation can be immense, yet this pressure is like the pressure that turns coal into diamonds.

I wish those of you who carry emanations from other worlds, both graciousness and great serendipity in your life on this interesting yet primitive planet. May your emanation be a blessing to Humanity and may your experience on Earth be a blessing to you.

Humanity has been granted free will as part of the evolvement of this dynamic universe. The choice before us now is to merge into a five-dimensional unity, knowing our souls are safe because, at that level, we already are inter-dimensional. So, given that Humanity chooses to join the multi-dimensional community, what can we look forward to?

[3]When Man makes his choice, he will discover whether he is to stay solid or move beyond such boundaries. Right now, it is only in death that Man rediscovers his true nature.

There you have it! As they say, what more can one aspire to? We do not need to pray to an external source. We are DIVINE, masquerading in human form as part of the Divine Master Plan. The truth is we are masters of our destiny. No God, or savior, is going to step in and save us; there is nothing to be saved.

I leave it to you to decide the truth and relevance of these revelations and how they might affect your point of view and reflect on the quote below.

The illiterate of the 21st century will not be those who cannot read and write, but those who cannot learn, unlearn, and relearn. —ALVIN TOFFLER[*‡‡‡]

---

‡‡‡ Alvin Toffler: (1928–2016). American writer and one of the world's outstanding futurists.

Free Will: A gift from The Divine

Free will is a unique gift from the Divine, granted to stimulate and accelerate our awareness. Our progress is observed with great interest by the multi-dimensional community.

The 11:11 ceremony in Egypt was mostly a celebration of free will. We opened a door in our consciousness to free us from our slavish dependence on prescriptive mandates about what we should believe. We took this first step by awakening our inherent sovereignty and recognizing our full potential: a subject covered in previous essays.

One of the great tragedies initiated by greed was the decimation of the New Worlds' indigenous people at the Spanish empire's hands. The karma created by the Old-World actions required an apology and a plea for forgiveness.

In 1992, a group of us intuited that the time was right to undertake a pilgrimage to the Mayan ruins in Palenque, Mexico, and offer that apology. The pyramid called the Temple of the Inscriptions houses the tomb of King Pakal, who ruled the Mayans around 680 AD. The elaborately carved image on the sarcophagus is said to depict his transition into divinity.

We held services of forgiveness and prayer in numerous sacred spots throughout the complex. A couple of days in, I could feel in my gut that it was my task, as a European, to offer this final plea. I had to do this alone, tell nobody, enter the pyramid, go to the tomb of Pakal, and bring closure for the terrible carnage visited on the Mayans.

As I descended, I became fully aware of the task before me. I had to petition out loud for forgiveness and offer myself as a sacrifice to heal the old wounds! Illuminated only by the light of three candles, the darkness felt solid! I have never been so scared, yet so confident about the service I was performing. I stood in front of the tomb, spread my arms, and spoke. The response was absolute silence; maybe it was wishful thinking, but I felt a sense of peace surge through me. Returning to the surface, I told my group, *"It is done: We have closure."*

I trembled with fear in that tomb, but my sense of purpose overcame instinct. I accessed my free will to help complete this service, for, *in my understanding,* I was in service to humankind.

As a sidebar, synchronicity played a big part in the success of that expedition. In Egypt, we had been granted sole occupancy of the whole site for three days. In Palenque, we had arrived, unknown to us, on Day One of a three-day local holiday; the local officials, however, granted us exclusive access to the site for three days. Both sites are worldwide attractions, and without that hiatus, it would have been impossible for either group to complete their missions.

If the task aligns with the good of the "universe," then the universe can pull dominant strings to get things done. I have had many divine interference examples in my personal life.

The "Pakal" experience was a glimpse into the multi-levels in which the central nervous system simultaneously operates. It reinforces my intention from the subtle information flowing in from multi-dimensional sources. The quote below encapsulates how I feel about this subject. Meryl Streep is an actor who has, in my opinion, optimized her potential. As a Master, she has achieved worldwide fame.

> *I'm in love with what I don't know. I'm in awe of what is not explainable or predictable.* —MERYL STREEP

Can you take on board that you are a multi-dimensional being, albeit in the early stages of evolvement, a human who has within, the capacity to be a way-shower on the path to multi-dimensionality?

[1]Free will, possessed by human beings as a precursor for the advancement of intelligence, is simply the way that God creates a challenge for them to develop stamina and poise. God does not need humans to have free will. They need free will for their own enjoyment, and thus it is granted to them:

The Divine does not judge or prescribe. We do have free will in how we travel this part of the journey because, in that context, what you do does not create a noticeable blip in the divine game plan.

The Cosmic "Rupert Bear" Annual

My earliest memory of seeing a rainbow was a colored drawing in my favorite children's storybook annual. A little bear, Rupert, was pictured riding to a new land on a rainbow. The prospect of being able to do that captured my imagination. Now! Decades later, my vision is on fire as I ride an exotic cosmic rainbow to a new mystery.

Throughout these essays, I have attempted to illustrate the part books and personal experiences played in laying the foundations of my passion for exploring spiritual teaching's mysteries. I am known as Mr. Woo-woo. It is not a flattering title, but you might find it entirely appropriate as my research's more exotic expressions unfold. Exotica constantly refuels my passion for the mysterious.

It seems that even at the highest levels of spiritual consciousness, mystery still lingers. The three statements below conjure up the "perfect storm of paradox" challenging God's omnipotence and upending the myth of an omnipotent God sitting on a throne in heaven.

> [1]*God can act as an advisor to time but cannot impose the act of volition or consciousness on to the laws that govern time.*

> [2]*Time no more than matter can change the mind of God, but it is time that ultimately determines the way that matter will be reshaped. Time recognizes the essential nature of God and, respectful of the understanding, exists concomitantly while being a witness of the Godforce as it emerges. This is the essential and mysterious paradox that underlies the formation of reality.*

Perhaps we need to demystify the gods? I realize that from a rational mainstream perspective, this undertaking could be a phantasmagoria of epic proportions. Although I profoundly resonate with the concepts presented, I do not have access to this cosmic level knowledge to form my own written descriptions. Therefore, I am going to rely on channeling from *The Reality of Time.*

> [3]*In the mythic stories of the gods, eternal beings take many forms. They can be humorous, wise, witty, quick to anger, unable to release their petty jealousies, or so keen to invoke punishment that their actions seem unjust or cruel. How can one live eternally without developing the basic mechanisms of compassion and justice that so moves the adult sentient being? The answer lies perhaps in the nature of the human mind itself. The capacity to learn, to grow, to struggle, and to die lends a certain nobility to human existence.*
>
> *It is not that eternal beings are exempt from such nobility, but they are not always willing to reach into the reservoir of creative intelligence and find the motivation for true loving-kindness.*
>
> [4]*One is often kind in human world through dictum, "Do unto others as you would have them done to you."*
>
> [5]*Eternal beings are very close to the expression of time. They are the closest attribute that the Godhead has created as an expression of what time actually is or could be. As a result, eternal beings have been worshiped by sentient life (which depends on sensory perception) in all portions of the universe.*

Although I cannot, as I have said, vouch for the accuracy of the above statements, my view leaves me in no doubt that we are part of a bigger cosmic game plan: a game that plays out in the realms of the infinite.

A rainbow forms when all seven colors unite. Similarly, humankind cannot evolve into a five-dimension civilization until we all join as ONE and the Godhead waits patiently to assess whether we are approaching that realization.

Marie Curie was a nurse, a tour de force, and a lightworker. And she was credited with delivering the following piece of wisdom relevant to the subject of this series of essays. Curie states:

> *I am amongst those who think that science has great beauty. A scientist in his (or her) laboratory is not a technician: he (or she) is also a child placed before natural phenomena which impress him (or her) like a fairy tale.*

I leave you to paint your reactions on the canvas of your reality.

Light: A Traveler and Messenger

Through my teens and twenties, the most influential and inspirational science fiction author was Arthur C. Clarke. Two books, *Childhood's End* and *The City and the Stars,* spoke about the evolution of Humanity and our expansion into the stars. My imaginative views and perspectives were molded from that base. Conversely, in 2006, I read *The Singularity Is Near* by Raymond Kurzweil˙§§§. His predictions filled me with a sense of déjà vu, that is, until I came to the chapter, which made a compelling argument for his belief that Humanity was alone in the Universe.

Kurzweil's evidence seriously challenged my cherished view and gave me a gut-churning realization that my whole cosmology would collapse if his theory were correct. Not to put too fine a point on it, I was traumatized for many months. Over time, I realized that elements were missing in Kurtzweil's argument. He had overlooked the probable existence of other dimensions,or levels of intelligent sentient lifeforms in different timelines.

[1]Light frequencies travel of their own accord separate from time and are not always tied to it. When matter becomes capable of separating from time, there is a process whereby the light value, which imbues matter with form, exists as a free-standing matrix.

[2]Since Light is a traveler, it has something to share, something to deliver. It is the seed package of illuminated consciousness. The planetary bodies, whether of Light duration or matter duration, retain a type of substance outside of linear time that makes their position in space/time transitory. They are the documenters of the celestial world. The planets develop a communications

---

§§§ Raymond Kurzweil is an American inventor and futurist. He has written books on health, artificial intelligence (AI), transhumanism, the technological singularity, and futurism. Wikipedia

highway from one-star system to another, encoding the plane-tary messages that signal the development of different starseed civilizations.

[3]*The God force recognizes the formation of planets and the star systems and makes sure that planets are coded with the light/ matter vestibules that develop free-standing intelligence.*

[4]*Once Beings become capable of utilizing light to further their exploration of interstellar space, they can actually calculate the range of light as it develops an interface with time.*

Absorbing humankind's scope and majesty requires a powerful sense of belonging and a vibrant vision of Humanity's potential. Our power comes through the exercise of love, authenticity, and self-respect. It comes from recognizing that all are equal, a *Cri de Coeur* uttered by the disadvantaged in many languages, to the point where it is now a cliché. In that sense, the sentiment is a beautiful example of hiding the truth in plain sight. The role the planets, as sentient beings, have in the development of matter and consciousness is breathtaking. I concede there is truth buried in the lore of Astrology. Until now, I never imagined that planets within a given system worked as a community to achieve the desires of the Divine.

To wind up this series of essays on Time and Light, I think the following quote by J.K. Rowling*[⸸⸸⸸] precisely strikes the right tone.

We do not need magic to change the world. We carry all the power we need inside ourselves already. We have the power to imagine better.

⸸⸸⸸   The British author best known for the Harry Potter novels

Psychology: The Mapping of Time

A friend who read my essays asked, "*Why are you trying to find explanations if everything that happens is magic?*"

We tend to use the word magic as a "back out" when faced with the inexplicable. Equally, even those who are open-minded and acknowledge that everything has an explanation can often be filled with awe and wonder when a slight crack in our reality bubble opens us to the Divine's ineffable mystery.

Astrophysicist Neil deGrasse Tyson***** declared, "*The universe is under no obligation to make sense to you.*" Bear his observation in mind when you read the quotes below. The question I asked myself was, *Does it feel right? Does it revitalize me at a deep level?*

> [1] *The flow of opposites that regulates the psychological experience of humanity is kept in place by the psychological constraints of the mind. Patterns of interaction between human beings are governed by the emotional intensity that is imposed by living in the duality of form. The event patterns that occur, though arising out of this emotional discontinuity, have a grace and efficacy to them that is not always easy to express.*

> [2] *The mapping is performed by beings whose Intelligence is intimately woven into their activities. They do not exist independently of time, but rather incorporate the motion of time within their awareness.*

> [3] *The algorithms that govern Time are formulated in stages to prevent a backup of information that would limit the*

**** *Neil deGrasse Tyson: a highly regarded American astrophysicist

development of this prehistorical point of view. Time beings of this magnitude often function in groups or pairs.

[4]*The indigenous mythologies which document stories of beings that must carry the weight of Time on their shoulders speak to these monumental activities.*

Can you imagine having an interaction with the map makers? The quote regarding our mythologies deeply embedded in all human cultures is enthralling. Understanding the myths' genesis helps create a thread, a glimpse of a web woven by ancient knowledge long forgotten. These stories continue to be regurgitated by each generation, each adding distortions reflecting their particular belief systems.

Today, the leading-edge theories in quantum mechanics espouse situations and probabilities that stretch our credibility and ability to grasp the basics. Here are a few examples.

Quantum entanglement: Is a methodology designed to transfer information instantaneously regardless of distance or location.

Quantum cryptography: When a particle is observed, it instantly changes as do all other entangled particles, like when one alters the value of a pixel and all other pixels that share the same address change. If information can be instantly sent through space-time, it means space-time is just a construct. In other words, there is a reality beyond our space-time illusion.

Quantum computing: Error correction codes maintain the integrity of qubits, the underlying mechanism for coherence.

Fractal geometry: Nature shares similar patterns.

Quantum indeterminate: Render what only needs rendering when observed.

One of the most startling conclusions drawn by scientists experimenting in the Quantum field is, to paraphrase, the observation of an event that defines the event's outcome that previously was in a place where all is possible. The best illustration of this phenomenon is the paradox raised by Erwin

Schrodinger* ††††in his thought experiment named Schrodinger's Cat: An unseen cat, in a box, is both dead and alive until it all is revealed when the box is opened!

We are on the brink of significant changes in our mainstream bodies of knowledge. There is always a fight to allow the light of the NEW to illuminate and update cherished, long-held beliefs. This last quote goes a long way to explain why.

> [5]Human memory must be approached delicately because its internal structure is filled with intelligent ghosts, afterburns of experience, contemplation, and reason. Since human beings are filled with many temporal tracks that have been garnered through lifetimes of wear and tear, it is up to the systematic organization of pure memory to keep everything centralized and available.

---

†††† Erwin Schrodinger: (1887–1961) Nobel Prize-winning Austrian-Irish physicist

Consciousness in Seismic Turmoil

Disturbed by my low energy levels, I decided to address the underlying cause; it was sadness underpinned by foreboding. In meditation, I asked my guides to shed some light on the matter. The floodgates opened, and a considerable download took place. The content was both visual, verbal, and wholly authoritative!

Use the movement of Earth's tectonic plates, by forces humans have no control over, as an analogy to highlight how little you understand or control the movement of the energy tectonic plates in your inner world.

There is an urgent need to pull Humanity out of the sinkhole of indifference about its future. There is an urgent need to wake up to the truism that all the problems in the world cannot be solved using or applying the same methodology that created them. Duality has been an essential tool in the learning and creation of civilization. Now the opportunity for Humanity to transcend into a mature, loving way of existence has never been so present and available. The answer is, to adopt one of your aphorisms, the solution will come out of the left field.

Earth's tectonic plates are in a state of constant dynamic flux. The timescale of these seismic events has allowed us to exist on the planet's surface under the illusion of stability. That illusion is now fragmenting. The destabilization of our environmental infrastructure is disrupting our mental and psychological landscape. In our inner world, a series of energetic tectonic plates, spiritual, subconscious, conscious, unconscious, imprinted events, intuition, and instinct, form a screen through which each of us perceives our reality.

All these plates have energetic signatures and switches which influence our behavior. As the energies of global awakening accelerate, our screens no longer present a picture of stability: It is like walking through the hall of distorting mirrors at a fairground. There is a complicated narrative in play, the details of which we can only guess. The voices of fear, hatred, greed, and isola-tion are in the ascendant and appear to have rendered us powerless to be pro-active. This strident symphony is the 'magnum opus'- the last great work, of the negative polarity whose job has been to disrupt the power of positive polarity.

One can only reflect on how powerful the positive force must be to elicit such a heavyweight response. The positive energy is available to all who choose to work from a heart-based template.

What stands in humanity's way, as a collective, applying the brakes to the "engines" of pollution "engines" like gasoline-fueled machines which ironically, we think, are vital for our survival? How does humanity measure up as spiritual entities in practicing what most spiritual/religious teaching advocates: love and compassion for all beings? Do we need to pay more atten-tion to "the Mother's" voice and cast aside the idea of dominion over land and beast?

The awakening of the feminine as a force for change and creation is still raw and fierce: it needs to be natural to break down many traditional prejudices.

Manifesting the answers to these questions would herald the dissolv-ing of the psychological shackles of this three-dimensional duality. The Gordian knot's legend comes to mind: What seemed to be a complicated intractable situation was solved by an unexpected source. One swing of Alexander's sword cut straight through the tightly entangled rope knot. Or, as Albert Einstein stated, *"No problem can be solved from the same level of consciousness that created it."*

Turning our vision inwards to become heart-based will enable us to access a new range of knowledge and understanding: an understanding that we indeed are masters of our destiny. In a follow-up download, this message came through.

There is no shortage of theories about the cataclysm that will either destroy or elevate humanity. All we can say is earthquakes, tsunamis, and epidemics create trauma that, through sheer terror, freezes people's ability to think in favorable terms. The event or events we envision will jolt humanity and cause an internal blast of fresh air to blow all the perception channels—inner channels that are presently blocked by the collective mindset's illusional conventions. As a result, the central nervous system will reawaken and be ready to receive multi-dimensional input.

Using state of the art technology, an international group of scientists*‡‡‡‡ has discovered what appears to be a substantial hidden chamber in the Great Pyramid. What might be in that chamber? There is speculation that it might be the ancient records of humanity's story? If true, it would cut through every mainstream theory about our origins in one stroke (Alexander's Sword).

What if these records confirm that previous human civilizations had contact with extra-terrestrials going back millions of years? The seismic shock would be immense, but then, as we would awaken out of the myth and illusion, our hearts would start to sing.

> [1]*This experiment in human encapsulation goes back many millions of years in Earth's history. It is now coming to a close in the years to come. There will be many beings that in the years to come will be returning to their natural, immortal, and timeless state. Such incarnations, as we see now will gradually become a thing of the past. This is not something that is being willed by human beings themselves; it is the will of God.*

Here is a footnote from my guides. *We invite all who read this message to step beyond the rational mind into a heart-based input process. This process will change your vibrational frequency to cope with the higher rates entering the planet's field. Please check whether what we say resonates with you before stepping forth.*

---

‡‡‡‡ Team to re-scan Great Pyramid of Giza to pinpoint hidden chamber. By SHINGO FUKUSHIMA/ Staff Writer. January 11, 2020.

The Divine Feminine/The Divine Mother

What is the Divine Feminine, and who is the Divine Mother? According to the mundane world's present gatekeepers, the Divine Feminine is just another New Age buzzword. I will return to this interpretation later.

In Christian cosmology, the Divine Mother is the mother of Jesus. In Buddhism, she has 21 forms but is known collectively as Tara, the mother of all Buddhas. In the Chinese Buddhist tradition, she is called Quan Yin. She manifests as Shakti in the Hindu tradition.

The oldest stone-aged artifact representing the feminine is a small statue of a heavy breasted full-bodied woman found in Willendorf in Austria, estimated to be over 30,000 years old. Below is a soupçon of her status drawn from the vast selection of written definitions and explanations.

According to Suzanne Kingsbury, author, and founder of Gateless Writing Inc., the Divine Feminine is the self-associated aspect with *creation, intuition, community, sensuality (felt sense rather than thinking sense), and collaboration.*

The Motherhood creates the Universe. Out of the Mother comes the Universe but it is the Father Principle that maintains everything in order in a particular situation. It has to, otherwise everything would collide and there would be total chaos in the Universe.

Swami Vivekananda, *Inspired Talks*, July 1895 explains:

The calm sea is the Absolute; the same sea in waves is Divine Mother. She is time, space, and causation. God is Mother and has two natures, the conditioned and the unconditioned. As the former, She is God, nature, and soul (humanity). As the latter,

She is unknown and unknowable. Out of the Unconditioned came the trinity god, nature, and soul, the triangle of existence... A bit of Mother, a drop, was Krishna, another was Buddha, another was Christ. The worship of even one spark of Mother in our earthly mother leads to greatness. Worship Her if you want love and wisdom.

The Reality of Time offers these fascinating snippets:

[1]*The Mother creates duality for Her amusement. She likes the play of light and dark, relishing in the interplay of shadow and form. The Mother enjoys the dialogue that happens when time must meet the dualistic and frozen version of itself as it rises from the absolute.*

[2]*Together, Mother and Father contribute to the hum that governs relative existence. They engender the pulse that keeps everything alive and in tune.*

Plainly from the dawn of human self-awareness, the feminine has had a well-defined role in human attempts to understand and appease the Gods. However, to fully embrace the Divine Feminine, we need to acknowledge the power she exercises in duality.

To achieve such an undertaking, we need to take onboard the assertion that there is a divine feminine aspect present in every sentient being. Our brain has two hemispheres. The right being the feminine, and the left the masculine. One side is usually dominant, and the interplay between the two creates duality, and the "right/wrong" discord evident in all our interactions. Stereotypically, we label males left-brained and females right-brained. This simplistic categorization leads to gender confusion. For instance, my gender is male, and my left-brain process has a big say in my decision making. I have worked hard to include the right-brain tools—intuition, compassion, patience, and love for all beings—in making decisions. Stripping power from both hemispheres' dominant extremes is part of the tough love needed to balance and ensure our existence. You may ask, *Aren't we God's chosen people?* That is a question best answered in this quote.

> [3]*We must understand that the Mother is the principal compositor of the time/space relationship between matter and absolute causation. Therefore, the Mother does not have the need of retaining anything which is fairly toothless and unfree. She will rip apart all of Her creation for the purpose of restitution.*

Tough love *indeed!*

Are We Aspiring to Freedom? Yes!

There is no doubt we are at a critical juncture. Are we ready to realize our true potential?

One of the most critical tributes we made at the 11:11 in Egypt happened in the Great Pyramid. The ceremony's purpose was to allow each participant to introduce themselves to the ancient elders present as guardians. A hundred-fifty folk made their way to the King's chamber entrance, deep inside the pyramid. Twelve of us held a short grounding meditation before inviting the first person to enter the room. We greeted the person and directed them to stand between the two rows of six facilitators. On prompt, they could speak or sing their Angelic name, receive a blessing, and exit. I was positioned in the middle, at the far end of the line, making sure that the sacred space was being held steady. As the chamber's energy heightened, I could clearly "see" a design develop on the stone floor.

"See" is an inadequate word to describe the fluency and depth of color in halos surrounding the lines pulsing before my eyes. I pinched myself. Yes! I was awake. Yet, I was in a location that most folk would judge to be ripe for free-ranging hallucinations. I felt a heightened sense of clarity come over me: the lines connected to interdimensional sources. An inner voice suddenly announced that groups had gathered across the world to act as local anchors to help the energies of evolution flow seamlessly into the Earth's energy field. Startling but unusual news—our mission to say farewell to the old and welcome the new powers of evolution was validated—this information was only for my ears. Free will demanded that each person needed to experience the effects of the new energies in their own time and step forward as their authentic self. Though it may sound vain of me right now, it is the first time the veil over this incident has fallen away, allowing me to recall my experience in its entirety.

In my timeline, the event lasted only minutes. However, the other facilitators told me they had been concerned because, for about twenty minutes, my body had been translucent, and I was incommunicado. Over the next two days, I felt disorientated, ungrounded, and puzzled. I was aware of being out-of-body and surrounded by priests of ancient Egypt but had no conscious details. Given the acceleration of change and confusion, it is appropriate to share as the old-world order dissolves.

One can never second guess the Divine. These essays have been an attempt to glimpse what I call the Divine perspective, focusing on where humanity stands in the Divine plan—a plan orchestrated by the Divine Mother. Given that the Mother is the genesis of creation's purpose, the quote below from an earlier essay that seemed hard-nosed at first read is perfectly understandable. Mother Earth is a sentient being, destined to follow her path of evolution. She will leave behind that which she does not want.

> *'The planetary intelligence is so strong, so mighty, and inviolate in its operating mechanics that, although it may appear damaged, it is rarely injured by the civilizations that act as matchbooks upon it. When the planet itself gets ready to ignite, it will take everything with it that is seemly and just leave behind that which it does not want.*

My optimism soars when I hear that sections of the scientific community are open to radical concepts. A new scientific concept has recently come to light, which scientists are calling "panpsychism."

The concept asserts that the Universe could be capable of consciousness, which, if true, could change everything. For quite some time, scientists have been working to understand the Universe, where it came from, and why we are here, and they have often come up short, until now!

The scientist responsible for such a notion is Gregory Matloff, and his ideas are shocking. According to Matloff, a professor of astronomy and physics at New York City College of Technology, "humans could be like the rest of the Universe, in substance and spirit." He proposes that a *proto-consciousness field* could extend throughout all space. Basically, in layman's terms, the entire cosmos could be self-aware. We can be part of the transition if we choose. How? Extend all-encompassing love to every element and aspect of yourself.

Embrace yourself as being part of the ONE regardless of your judgments about yourself. That is my plan and intention.

NAMASTE

Epilogue

In the Spring of 2018, my resistance to 'stepping out' was finally overcome by a nagging sense of urgency: the change was accelerating. Alarm bells were ringing all around the world regarding our planet's health, and the human collective seemed unwilling to address the issue—a situation which, if not managed, would have dire consequences for our civilization. The spiritual community consensus was that we needed to rise out of the fog of illusion. This message was like a flashing neon sign in my awareness. The material you have just finished reading resulted from input from higher Intelligence and the escalation of my self-awareness.

In February of 2020, 'COVID 19' stamped the word CHANGE on every aspect of our lives. The shock wave that hit me was intense and instant. It is all very well professionally writing about the inevitability of drastic change in the future tense. As I write, I am experiencing the pain of loss, and in contradiction, a sense of excitement:

I believe that even as our civilization moves into the winter of its old values, a Spring and Summer full of new potential awaits us if we are prepared to write a new narrative for living compassionately. 'COVID 19' forces each of us to question our values and priorities.

The grief about the death of my expectations came in waves: like all revelations, simple ones can devastate the most. My plans for traveling to the UK are rescheduled for May 2021. Reviewing these plans, I realized, I had automatically made assumptions based on previous trips. I would stay with the same dear friends, visit this person, spend some time exploring this location, etc. Would I, Could I? I froze as a whole new understanding spread through my awareness, '*The only certainty is what is happening in the present moment*.' This reality has always been so. But we have had the luxury of projecting the illusion of stability into the past and future. The past is gone and is irrelevant as a planning tool for the future. The 'future' is just a series of potentialities.

Initially, the void this opened up in me was disorientating. I was in freefall. Slowly a new self-awareness opened like a parachute. I landed in the vast potential of the present moment. What do I mean by the vast potential of the present moment?

Two weeks before lockdown, I was in my usual busy coffee shop. There only two spaces available. I chose one and put my cup down when an internal voice said, "No, sit at the one behind that!" I listen to my intuition, so I moved. Half an hour later, I looked up from my writing about quantum physics and saw a young woman sitting next to me, immersed in typing. There was a book on the table close to her. Curious, I glanced to see its title, but I could only read the word Quantum. I asked what she was studying, "*Human Design*" she responded.

That was the start of collaboration and firm friendship. Recently I sought Kelly's permission to include this story in this Epilogue as it was a great example of the vast potential of the present moment. She agreed but was insistent that the word Quantum was not on the cover of her book. "*I can see that book cover with the word on it in my mind's eye.*" Her explanation: "*Sometimes, the universe uses the most appropriate tool for the job, and you saw what was needed to draw you forward.*"

'*All will unfold as it should, or not!*' (ANON)

Contribute to the Narrative

"The illiterate of the 21st century will not be those who cannot read and write, but those who cannot learn, unlearn, and relearn." —ALVIN TOFFLER-FUTURIST.

I invite you to join in a dialogue. Your perspective is essential and necessary if we want to create a community that supports open-minded, self-aware input. You are not alone. Lonely sometimes, yes, but I am confident you embrace the potential of self-awareness and are ready to help create a new narrative for humanity.

To start our conversation, please consider the four questions below. I would love to read your responses and answer any questions that arise. I am interested in the words belonging and acceptance. What do they mean to you?

Belonging can mean be own or to be part of something greater than ourselves. The latter is often not a conscious choice. You can belong to a family yet not be accepted by them. Acceptance is part of belonging, but belonging does not necessarily mean you are accepted!

1. *We all belong to a specific DNA group. Statistically, my DNA can predict how I will be disposed to act in certain conditions and provide indicators about my short and long-term health expectations. Do you think we can alter our genetic patterns as Quantum Science asserts?*

2. *Have you ever consciously chosen acceptance, like suspending the judgment of others? If so, what method would you recommend?*

3. *For this discussion, let us say that belonging to the human race was not a conscious choice. And, being born into your family was not a*

conscious choice. If you agree with these assertions, have you found them easy to accept, or do you feel limited by these factors?

4. *We are capable of self-sacrifice. Are such impulses an expression of our built-in compassion and awareness of serving the overall good?*

Please send your responses to, <u>kenasheville3@gmail.com</u>

Thank you. I look forward to hearing from you.

Blessings

Kenneth A Macfarlane

References

Page sources of quotations drawn from *The Reality of Time* by Janet Iris Sussman.

All Depends on Your Point of View

1,2. *The Reality of Time*, page: 88

3. *The Reality of Time*, page: 04

Earth: An Independent Sentient Being

1,2. *The Reality of Time*, page: 129

3,4. *The Reality of Time*, page: 130

Our Status as a Civilization

1. *The Reality of Time*, page: 130

Golem and Pygmalion

1. *The Reality of Time*, page:138

Synchronicity: A Tool of the Divine

1. *The Reality of Time*, page:178

Ripening the Fruit of Devotion and Surrender

1. *The Reality of Time*, page:269

Doorways to Cognition

1. *The Reality of Time*, page:230

No "Me": The Gift of Surrender?

1. *The Reality of Time*, page:143

2. *The Reality of Time*, page:143

Breath: The Elixir of Awakening

1. *The Reality of Time*, page:182

2. *The Reality of Time*, page:185

3. *The Reality of Time*, page:182

Memory: The Storehouse of Our Reality

1. *The Reality of Time*, page:155

2. *The Reality of Time*, page:155

3. *The Reality of Time*, page:156

Human Beings Are Simply…?

1. *The Reality of Time*, page:202

The Potential of Our Children Part 1 of 2

1. *The Reality of Time*, page:213

2. *The Reality of Time*, page:141

The Potential of Our Children Part 2 of 2

1,2. *The Reality of Time*, page:213

SPECIAL QUOTES

The Reality of Time, page:214

Children experiencing "learning disorders" often have difficulty in conforming to the strictures of a rigid dimensional time reference. They are actually seeing or hearing information from an interdimensional time source and are seeking to make sense out of such information from a three-dimensional reference point.

The Reality of Time, page:214

These children are often high-functioning inter-dimensional emissaries, but due to misunderstanding and improper identification of them on a soul level, they are bound to encounter difficulties within the present education system. It would be beneficial to develop a course of study starting in elementary school about the nature of time and consciousness. These demand that the instructors be highly knowledgeable themselves.

Developing the flow of Awareness

1. *The Reality of Time*, page:227

"Aha" Moments and Assumptions

1,2. *The Reality of Time*, page:222

The Body: A Biochemical Marvel

1.2. *The Reality of Time*, page:209

Initiation, Purpose, and Eternity

1,2. *The Reality of Time*, page:313

Factors of Human Personality

1,2,3. *The Reality of Time*, Page.220

Patience: The Lifeblood of Beauty and Order

1. *The Reality of Time*, page:221

Awakening the Language of Awareness

1. *The Reality of Time*, page:236

2. *The Reality of Time*, page:234

The Limits of the Ego

1. *The Reality of Time*, page:240

Celestial Plans Are Infinitely Variable

1. *The Reality of Time*, page:258

Male and Female: The Universal Mystery!

1,2. *The Reality of Time*, page:259

The Liquidity of Awareness

1. *The Reality of Time*, page:266

Are We Aspiring to Freedom? YES!

The Reality of Time, page:130

Epilogue

1. Human Design: Extracted from, jovianarchive.com

   Human Design offers a map of your unique genetic design, with detailed information on both conscious and unconscious aspects of yourself. Using simple tools, it guides you in discovering your own truth. If you suffer from a lack of self-love or clarity about your purpose and the direction of your life, this system can help.

   When you come to Human Design as an adult, it has the potential to awaken your innate wisdom and power. Your process of awakening to your true self requires two things: Education and Experimentation. For an adult, the road back to living life as yourself can be challenging overcoming life-long habits and the power of conditioning takes commitment, courage, and determination.

   You need to experiment with your Design and find what is right for you. To be what you are not—to live the conditioning—leads to dis-ease as you continually confront energies you are not genetically equipped to handle. Human Design is a tool that can help you understand how your body and mind are meant to run properly, and how to align with others who can support your process.

1. Kelly Studer.

   Is a coach specializing in the transformative power of 'Human Design'. kellystuder.com

Afterword

In the Preface, i stated my purpose was to share from a neutral loving space: a challenging aspiration to sustain because it is easy to jump out of my heart space when the pain of outrage pulls me back into anger and judgment.

We, as a civilization, are at a choice point. Are we ready to raise our awareness and embrace heartfelt values? The consequences of failure are dire, as illustrated throughout these essays. However, I am confident the human heart's generous impulse will provide us with the energy and courage to move forward.

Early in 2019, I downloaded a channeling regarding a pending grand-scale event that would create the impulse in humankind to examine the current values we apply to our lives and the broader community's well-being. I never imagined that a year later, the world would be under the hammer of a pandemic. It would be an easy shot for me to say I told you so.

Please commit to raising your game. Use your God-given gift of self-awareness. Embrace the need to implement a heart-based approach in dealing with all sentient life. Please recognize we cannot sustain ourselves as a species without the cooperation of Mother Earth.

Each person reading these words is a lightworker. I salute you because your perspective is broad enough to support those immersed in fear and confusion. Have compassion: They cannot see or perceive any light or redemption. Our job is not to preach or fix. Our task is to be clear and bright, so others project whatever fear it does not find a toehold in our energy field. Your neutral and calm presence will allow them time for some reconsideration. That is all you need to be.

You are needed; you are not alone, though it is highly likely you feel lonely as all the old paradigm themes drop away. That too shall pass.

BLESSINGS!